Toward a Post-Biblical Christian Future

Toward a Post-Biblical Christian Future

RICK HERRICK

WIPF & STOCK · Eugene, Oregon

TOWARD A POST-BIBLICAL CHRISTIAN FUTURE

Wipf & Stock
An Imprint of Wipf and Stock Publishers
199 W. 8th Ave., Suite 3
Eugene, OR 97401

www.wipfandstock.com

PAPERBACK ISBN: 979-8-3852-2642-9
HARDCOVER ISBN: 979-8-3852-2643-6
EBOOK ISBN: 979-8-3852-2644-3

07/19/24

For Bob, with profound appreciation.

Contents

Acknowledgments

I WANT TO BEGIN by thanking my old friend Diane Dreher. I came to know Diane forty years ago when she was a regular contributor to a magazine I edited. Diane has had a distinguished career as an English professor, college administrator, and, in her current position, as associate director of the Applied Spirituality Institute at Santa Clara University. Among her many publications are three pathbreaking books on Taoism. Diane provided amazingly insightful criticism on early drafts of this book.

I also want to thank Bob Coe for our lifelong friendship. Bob had a distinguished career in the foreign service as an economist with postings in Bolivia, Ghana, Chile, and India. In the United States, he worked at the State and Commerce Departments. After retiring, he began a second career, teaching forty-nine courses in a wide variety of subjects for the Osher Lifelong Learning Institute at American University.

Bob was my walking buddy for more than forty years. He was the best-read person I have ever encountered. He enlightened me on a wide variety of subjects. Even more importantly, he provided thoughtful criticism on almost everything I have written. Sadly, he died just as I was finishing *Toward a Post-Biblical Christian Future.* Had he been able to read an early draft of the book, I feel certain it would have been much improved.

Bob was gentle, soft-spoken, a great listener, thoughtful, and a loyal friend. He defined for me what it means to be a good human being. It is therefore my great honor to dedicate this book to his memory.

Finally, I want to thank the Wipf and Stock staff for their friendly cooperation in putting this project together and for their considerable help with editing the final draft. I have worked with five publishing houses, and this group is in a league of their own.

Introduction

THIS IS A DIFFICULT book for me to write. Fifty-five years ago, an Introduction to the New Testament class in college changed my life. I became fascinated intellectually with the Bible. It's a fascination which led me to give up a tenured university professorship in political science. I have spent the last forty years reading deeply into the literature of the Old and New Testament. Sadly, I have recently come to a different conclusion regarding the Bible. I now see it as a major problem for the Christian religion, a stumbling block when it comes to knowing God in a deep experiential sense.

This will be a difficult book for most Christians to read because the Bible has been the anchor to their faith for the last 1,900 years, but Christianity is dying in the West. When Lyn and I travel to Western Europe, the churches we come across have become museums. Active church membership, as defined by attending religious services at least once a month, has declined in Western Europe to 22 percent of the population.[1]

This decline has also come to America. The Gallup polling organization first began to measure church membership in 1937. At that time, 73 percent of Americans were members of a church, a figure that remained steady for the next sixty years. Yet today only 47 percent of Americans claim church membership. This decline will likely continue because church membership is strongly correlated with age. In 2021, only 36 percent of millennials claimed to be

1. Tornielli, "Statistics on the Slow Evaporation of European Christianity," para. 2.

xi

members of a church.[2] As a result of this decline, a 2021 study from Lifeway Research listed 4,500 church closings in 2019, with only 3,000 new openings. Average worship attendance in US churches declined from 137 people to 65 people in the last two decades. On an average Sunday, only 22 percent of Americans attend church. If you take out the South, that number declines to 10 percent.[3]

There are many reasons for this rapid decline, but a major one is belief. Many people are no longer finding the beliefs outlined in the Bible believable. As a result, it's time we had a conversation about it. It is my hope that this book will help to begin that conversation. The first two chapters will examine the causes of why the Bible, from the perspective of the twenty-first century, has become outdated and a hindrance to a healthy spirituality. Chapter three will look at the consequences that have followed from the two-thousand year history of Christianity as a religion of belief. Chapter four will explore ways we can redefine the Christian faith. Note that the title of the book does not suggest fixing these problems. This is not a book about reinterpreting the Christian Bible to make it more relevant for the modern era; rather, it is about a better way to become a follower of Jesus by finding a new anchor for the Christian faith.

A few explanatory notes are necessary before we get started. I will use traditional notations for Jewish and Christian scriptures because I find the terms Old Testament and New Testament more specific and less likely to lead to confusion. By adopting this strategy, I do not imply in any way that Christian scriptures represent a higher form of revelation than Jewish scriptures. They both have considerable problems from the perspective of our age, which will become clear in the pages that follow. I will, however, use CE for "common era," which replaces AD, and BCE for "before the common era," a replacement for BC.

Fifty-five years ago I purchased the Jerusalem Bible for the New Testament class I mentioned above. Our professor chose this Bible because it was written in plain English, with introductions for

2. Frishberg, "American Church Membership Hits Historic Low."
3. Smietana, "Thousands of Churches Close Every Year."

each book and explanatory notes scattered throughout. The Gospel references cited in this book come from the Jerusalem Bible.

Finally, you will quickly notice biblical references follow many of the points made in the book. It is important for you to check these references, especially if you come across something you don't understand or have difficulty agreeing with me. To check the scriptural reference against the point I am making will greatly enhance its impact. Because I know most of you won't do that, I'm going to make an offer. I will pay anyone one hundred dollars if they discover a passage I have misused or misrepresented.

I make this offer because I want readers to have confidence in the passages I cite, but there are two qualifications. First, I will only pay the first person who discovers the problem. I can't afford someone ganging up on me and telling all his friends, "Hey, let's get this guy." Second, if I can show the point I am making conforms with mainline biblical scholarship, I will write a letter listing authors that support my position, which will not include a check. Please email me at rherrick86@gmail.com with questions or any problems you discover. I look forward to hearing from you.

1

A Very Human Book

BISHOP ATHANASIUS OF ALEXANDRIA was the father of the Christian canon. In a letter to fellow bishops in 367 CE, Athanasius listed twenty-seven books that became the New Testament. As a result, the New Testament as we know it came into existence more than three hundred years after the crucifixion of Jesus.

Not long after Athanasius's letter, Saint Augustine, the bishop of Hippo and an early Christian theologian, pronounced this canon to be completely free from error. These twenty-seven books were informed by the mind of God. Every word came from God. Augustine's solution to the inerrant New Testament canon lasted for more than a thousand years. Conservative Christians today honor it with few exceptions. The purpose of this chapter is to point out the problems with the idea that the Christian Bible is the inerrant word of God, that in fact it is a very human book. We will begin by looking at some glaring contradictions found in both the Old and New Testaments.

GLARING CONTRADICTIONS

The Creation Stories

It is appropriate to start with the creation stories because that's where the Bible begins. It will surprise many Christians to learn that there are in fact two stories. The first story runs from Gen 1:1 through Gen 2:4, while the second story begins with verse 2:5 and continues through chapter 3. You don't have to be a biblical scholar to recognize the two stories are totally different.

To begin with, the order of creation is different in each story. God's first day is devoted to creating light in the first story. Humans don't make the scene until day six. In the second story, the first thing created is a human being named Adam. There is no Adam or Eve in the first story. Read the two stories for yourself and list the order of creation for each story. The differences are stark and intriguing.

The picture of God in the two stories is remarkably different. God creates by his word in the first story. He is separate from the world and humans, fully in control, majestic, and transcendent. The God of the second story is far more human. He interacts with Adam and Eve, and he creates with his hands from within the world. God the potter of the second story replaces the majestic God of the universe in story number one.

If you read the two stories in their entirety, other differences appear. The attitude toward women is different. In the first story, male and female are created equally. In the second story, Adam comes first. Eve is eventually created from Adam's rib because God decides Adam needs a companion and a helpmate. When Eve makes the fateful decision to eat the forbidden fruit, the die is cast for women according to the traditional Christian interpretation of the story. Eve was not only second-born; she was the first to sin. We can't ignore the implications of this second story. It has been a major factor in keeping women as second-class citizens in many Christian churches and within American society generally.

In like manner, the philosophy that directs each story is different. Everything God created in story number one is good, including human beings who are patterned on the divine image. The second story is more complex. For many Christians, this is the story where Adam and Eve fall from God's good graces because of Eve's decision to sample the forbidden fruit. Humans are not so good in story number two.

Finally, for those of you who are theologically inclined, spend some time reflecting on chapter 1, verse 26. The author of the first story does not seem to posit an absolute monotheism. God, the king, has a cabinet of lesser deities who help him do his work. From a Christian perspective, the second story is preferred because God is seen as one.

The differences noted above indicate there are no common elements in the two stories. Each story has a different author. If you believe Genesis provides a historic account of creation, at minimum one of the stories is fictional. As an optimist, I have always voted for the first story where everything God created was good. If you deny climate science because of a belief that these first three chapters of Genesis provide historically accurate information, it is time for you to reconsider your position.

The Ten Commandments

In 2017, fundamentalist firebrand Roy Moore's loss to Democrat Doug Jones for the Senate seat vacated by Attorney General Jeff Sessions in Alabama brought the Christian Bible front and center into the political debate. Judge Moore first came to my attention in August of 2001 when he erected a monument to the Ten Commandments on the rotunda of Alabama's state judicial building. That was a nice gesture, but the problem is that Jewish Scripture contains two different sets of Ten Commandments.

Let me briefly review the Moses story. In chapter 20 of Exodus, God gives the people of Israel Judge Moore's Ten Commandments, the Ten Commandments we all know and love. In chapter 24, the people ratify the covenant Moses made with God, and Moses returns to the mountain to receive the stone tablets. Chapters

25 through 31 cover instructions God gave Moses for the building of the sanctuary and the behavior of priests.

The story of the Ten Commandments resumes in chapter 32 of Exodus. Because Moses was away for a long time, the people construct a golden calf as an aid for their worship. When Moses returns and sees the golden calf, he explodes with anger, throwing the tablets at the golden calf, which destroys both the idol and the tablets. God is angry too and wants to end his relationship with the people of Israel.

Over time both God and Moses calm down, and God invites Moses back to the mountain to receive new tablets. In chapter 34 of Exodus, God promises to inscribe the exact same ten laws onto tablets and then for some reason changes his mind. God ends up giving Moses ten different laws as his Ten Commandments. Judge Moore's monument missed God's final word on the subject.

Defenders of the faith will claim that this second set of commandments does not contain the important ones, that the commandments in chapter 20 of Exodus are the ones with universal significance. The problem with this argument is that God spells out how he wants to be worshiped in the second set, a foundational statement defining the religion for the people of ancient Israel.

The Question of a King

My favorite contradiction in the Old Testament comes in 1 Samuel. The book contains two traditions. The first tradition sees Samuel as a prophet who provides advice on a wide range of issues. Because the Philistines are threatening, he recommends that the people of Israel establish a monarchy as a means of protection. He is eventually commissioned by God to anoint Saul as king (1 Sam 9:16–17).

The second tradition pictures Samuel as a judge, a ruler of the people but near the end of his life. While the people clamor for a king to protect them from the Philistines, Samuel refuses to accede to their demands because only God can be king (1 Sam 8:4–15).

There were two branches of Judaism in ancient Palestine. Galilee to the north had a strong history of independence.[1] They were only controlled by Jerusalem during the reigns of kings David and Solomon, as well as that of the Hasmoneans. King Solomon died in 931 BCE, and the Hasmoneans finally extended their control over Galilee in 104 BCE. That gave the Galileans eight hundred years of independence from Jerusalem. Although they were ruled by colonial masters from time to time, foreign control was distant and largely ineffective.

A tradition of self-reliance and independence was protected for Galileans by the rugged terrain, isolated villages, and the fact that these villages were located a long way from navigable waterways. In contrast to Judea to the south, there were no overarching institutions or an aristocratic ruling class. Galilee was a land of mostly free landowners who resented the rule of kings David and Solomon because they were taxed, conscripted to serve in the army, and forced to labor in building the temple and the palaces of wealthy Jews in Jerusalem.

Jesus' Galilean heritage helps to explain his central teaching of the coming of God's kingdom. In all of his teachings on God's kingdom, no Messiah is promised or even mentioned with regard to bringing in this kingdom. This is a kingdom where God will rule. Isaiah, Jesus' favorite prophet, agreed with him that only Yahweh could be king (see Isa 33:22; 43:15; 44:6; 52:7).

The Virgin Birth of Jesus

Moving to the New Testament with the two virgin birth stories, the starting point for understanding them is to read them both carefully (see Matt 1:18—2:23 and Luke 1:26—2:39). When you do this, write down the main events in each story. Here is what I find when I go through this process.

In Matthew, the story begins with Mary and Joseph residing in Bethlehem. We quickly learn that Mary is with child as a result

1. See Horsley, *Galilee.*

of some mysterious intervention by the Holy Spirit. Jesus is born in Bethlehem and visited by wise men. Because it was believed that a king of the Jews had been born, the current king, Herod, is threatened. He instructs the wise men to go to Bethlehem to locate Jesus so that he could make a similar journey to pay his respects. The wise men find Jesus by following a star, which seems to wander around in the universe. While with the family, the wise men offer gifts and have a dream telling them to return home a different way to avoid reporting to Herod. Soon after they leave, Joseph has a dream telling him to escape to Egypt with Mary and Jesus. In anger and frustration, because he was unable to locate the baby Jesus, Herod kills all male children in the surrounding area under two years of age. When Herod dies, an angel again appears to Joseph, informing him it is now safe to leave Egypt. The family travels to Nazareth.

In Luke, the story begins with Zechariah and Elizabeth, the parents of John the Baptist. Elizabeth conceives John the Baptist as a result of a miracle. In this case, God solves a fertility problem. The angel Gabriel explains to Mary that she will also have a child, conceived by the Holy Spirit. Mary visits her cousin Elizabeth. She sings the Magnificat, and John is born. The story now moves to the birth of Jesus in earnest. Caesar Augustus orders a census, which causes Mary and Joseph to make the trip from Nazareth to Bethlehem. Note that they reside in Nazareth. Mary gives birth while in Bethlehem at an inn witnessed by shepherds. Jesus is circumcised at the temple, and the family returns to Nazareth.

Most Christians do not make such an outline. They conflate elements from both stories, and this composite picture is reinforced every Christmas when the Christmas pageant is performed in their church. However, if you are honest and objective in your examination of the two stories, it jumps out at you that the two stories have nothing in common. One is the story of the birth of a king with a star wandering around the universe, wise men visiting, children dying, and a trip to Egypt. The story in Luke is about the birth of a Palestinian peasant in a simple inn with shepherds in attendance and a quick turnaround home to Nazareth. One of these stories must be fiction.

In fact, both stories are fiction. Why? To begin with, Paul never mentions a virgin birth in any of his letters. Paul is one of the greatest salesmen in history. If a virgin birth happened, he would have proclaimed it in every letter he wrote. Instead, Paul hints in both Romans (1:3–4) and Galatians (4:4) that the birth of Jesus occurred through normal human processes.

Mark never mentions a virgin birth. John also fails to mention it. The author of John suggests in chapter 6 that Jesus was born through normal human processes. In chapter 1, he indicates that Jesus was born in Nazareth (1:45–56. See also John 7:42). The virgin birth of Jesus is nowhere mentioned in a history of the period nor in any other New Testament documents. Think about the claim—virgin birth. It's an amazing one with no independent historical confirmation. In all of world literature, the claim is made only in Matthew and Luke.

> "Surely this is Jesus, son of Joseph," they said. "We know his mother and father." (John 6:42)

There are also historical problems with the two stories. The census mentioned in Luke never took place. The evangelist uses it as a device to get Mary to Bethlehem so that the birth will confirm the prophecy of Micah (5:2)—an example of prophecy creating history, a tactic often used by the evangelists in creating their stories. To repeat, the worldwide census never took place. There was a smaller one in Syria, however, when Jesus was ten.

Can you imagine an eight-months-pregnant woman walking five or six days to get to Bethlehem? How about the star that wanders around the universe or the wise men who make a long journey to honor the birth of a Galilean peasant? These elements of Matthew's story stretch my imagination.

Bethlehem was seven miles from Jerusalem, the home of Herod. Why did Herod have to ask wise men for help in locating Jesus in this tiny village? And then there's the killing of all those children. History reports that Herod killed a few of his own kids, but there is no record of an atrocity like the one described in Matthew.

Finally, stories of miraculous births were common in ancient literature for great men. Such stories were written for Moses, Samuel, John the Baptist, Apollonius of Tyana, Alexander the Great, Romulus, Augustus Caesar, to name a few. Do we believe these stories?

The Resurrection of Jesus

Amazingly, the evangelists do not agree as to where the resurrection took place. Matthew places it on a mountain in Galilee (28:16–20) and Luke at a home in Jerusalem (24:33–43). The distance between these two points of reference is a five- or six-day walk. John agrees with Luke regarding the Jerusalem home (20:19–29) but adds a resurrection encounter on the shores of Lake Tiberias in Galilee (21:1–19). No other Gospel mentions this encounter at the lake, a rather significant omission if eyewitnesses authored these accounts.

> Later on Jesus showed himself again to the disciples.
> It was by the sea of Tiberias. (John 21:1–2)

Some try to reconcile these different accounts by positing that Jesus first appeared to the disciples in Jerusalem and only later in Galilee. Unfortunately, Luke's story makes such a solution impossible. According to Luke, Jesus appeared in Jerusalem and immediately afterward ascended to heaven.

There are also differences pertaining to the form of Jesus' resurrection. For Matthew, Luke, and John, the form was physical. Jesus rose from the dead, walked on the earth, and ate with his disciples. In contrast, the resurrection for Paul was a vision experience. Paul had a vision of Jesus in heaven as he was traveling on the road to Damascus (see Acts 9:1–9 and Acts 26:12–17). There is no hint in either text that Jesus appeared to Paul in a physical body on earth. In 1 Cor 15:3–8, Paul insists his resurrection experience was the same as the experiences of the disciples.

Discrepancies of this magnitude are hard to forgive. We are talking about the most spectacular event ever alleged to have taken place in human history. Where was President Kennedy assassinated? Few people living in 1963 would have differing views about that. A physical encounter and a vision experience have nothing in common.

Gospel Organization

There is a general consensus among New Testament scholars that Mark was the first Gospel to be written. His Gospel is organized around a one-year ministry with a last week in Jerusalem for the Passover festival. The crucifixion and resurrection take place during that week. Matthew and Luke follow Mark's organization scheme.

You can't read the Gospel of John without noticing how different it is from the Synoptic Gospels of Mark, Matthew, and Luke. One notable difference is that John's Gospel is organized around a three-year ministry, with Jesus setting out three times to attend the Passover festival (John 2:13; 5:1; 7:10). There is little debate among New Testament scholars regarding the two organizational schemes. The two different organizational schemes make it difficult to posit inerrant construction of the Gospel texts.

The Last Words of Jesus

Mark is believed to be the primary author of the passion narrative for the Synoptic Gospels. He and Matthew have very similar stories. Both evangelists present Jesus as being abandoned by his followers and God. His prayer is not answered at Gethsemane, and his disciples flee when he is arrested. He faces the cross alone and agonizes over it. His last words before dying in both Gospels are "My God, my God. Why have you deserted me?" (Mark 15:34; Matt 27:47).

The picture is different in Luke. In Luke, Jesus appears as a stoic, quietly accepting his fate. He praises his disciples for standing by him, (22:28–30), and his prayer is answered at Gethsemane (22:44). There are no expressions of anguish in Luke. Jesus' last words on the cross are "Father, into your hands I commit my spirit" (Luke 23:46).

With John, the events are different from Mark's listing. John has no triumphant entry into Jerusalem on a colt, no Gethsemane scene, no temple confrontation, and no trial before the Sanhedrin. In John's story, Jesus is pictured as the stage director. He controls the arrest scene where he greets Judas. When he identifies himself to the Roman soldiers, they fall down in awe and reverence. In a real sense, Jesus allows them to arrest him. He dominates the meeting with Pilate. His last words on the cross say it all: "It is accomplished" (John 19:30).

The three brief summaries of the passion narratives in Mark, Luke, and John above note several interesting historical differences among the three accounts. When you compare similar Gospel stories in this way, such differences are almost always found. What interests me here, however, is the three different versions of Jesus' last words on the cross. At minimum two evangelists put words into Jesus' mouth. This is a freedom the evangelists exercise frequently when writing their Gospel stories. Such a practice strongly supports the conclusion that these stories were created by human beings and do not represent the inerrant word of God.

A quick look at the Gospel of John will help to drive this point home. In the second section of the Gospel referred to as the book of Signs (1:19 through chapter 12), there are seven miracle stories which are followed by a sermon by Jesus. These sermons have a distinct pattern. Most begin with a statement by Jesus which is misunderstood. Jesus then proceeds to explain his answer in a long speech. Most of the sermons have no eyewitnesses present, there were certainly no recording devices, and no one is seen taking notes. You don't memorize a long speech by listening to it. It's rather evident that the evangelist got these speeches from some written source and attributed the words to Jesus.

The same tactic is used in creating the third section of the Gospel known as the book of Glory (John 13:1–17:20). In these three chapters, Jesus gives a farewell address to his disciples which amounts to an extended monologue on mutual love. It is one of the most beautiful presentations in the New Testament. Its length, and the fact that only the disciples were present who were illiterate peasants, suggest that the words come from someone other than Jesus. The evangelist who wrote John seventy or more years after this alleged meeting took place had no qualms about putting words in the mouth of Jesus.

In 1985 Robert Funk founded the Jesus Seminar, a group of distinguished scholars who meet periodically to determine the authenticity of the words of Jesus. By their estimate after several years of study and debate, only 20 percent of the words attributed to Jesus in the four Gospels are likely to be authentic.[2] If this estimate is even close to being accurate, the question naturally arises as to whether we can have confidence in the biblical record with regard to our understanding of the historical and post-resurrection Jesus.

PROBLEMATICAL PREDICTIONS

The Classical Prophets

We now move to an examination of the problematical predictions made in both the Old and New Testaments beginning with the classical prophets. The classical prophets—Amos, Hosea, Isaiah, Jeremiah, and Ezekiel—are one of Israel's great gifts to Western civilization. From the prophets we acquire profound insights into the practice of religion. From Deutero-Isaiah (Isa 40–55), we have the eloquent poetry that speaks to the power of innocent suffering as a way to lead one to God. From Jeremiah, my favorite, we learn that the old covenant has been annulled due to disobedience but that a new covenant will be granted based on circumcision of the heart. Religion will no longer be about external laws written on

---

2. See Funk and Hoover, *Five Gospels*.

tablets of stone but about an inward, moral sense of the living God. Judge Roy Moore, are you listening?

We owe these prophets a lot, and yet, as you will see, they are not great predictors. Actually, to be fair, prediction was not the role assigned to them by God. Rather, they were specifically chosen by God to speak his word. The word of God entered into them, which they then proclaimed. "Thus, Yahweh speaks" precedes many of their oracles.

Evangelical Christians claim that no Jewish scriptural prophecy has gone unfulfilled. This presumed fact proves the divine authority of the Bible, that God wrote it. In predicting the future, the prophets did not err. They spoke the word of God.[3]

In *The Case Against Evangelical Christianity*, I examined this claim that the prophets spoke the word of God in detail. I listed every time one of the five prophets mentioned above spoke the word of God and then determined whether that word actually came true in history. The findings are stark. Less than 10 percent of their statements materialized in history in a meaningful way. To make the point for this section of the chapter, I don't have to present the results of the entire study. A summary of Jeremiah's utterances of the word of God should do. Readers interested in the full study can consult my book.[4]

Jeremiah is the prophet of Judah's (the Southern Kingdom) decline and fall. He receives his call in 627 BCE. In Jer 3:14–18, he foresees a glorious future for Jerusalem in which the north/south split is healed and all nations gather there in Yahweh's name. It is Yahweh who speaks. The north/south split occurred following the death of Solomon when Israel was divided into two parts. There has been no time in history when this split was healed under Israel's sovereignty with the exception of Hasmonean rule from 104 BCE until the Roman conquest in 63 BCE—forty-one years over the course of a three-thousand-year history.

The prophet also promises that the "Branch of David" will rule again in Jerusalem as true king. That never happened.

---

3. McDowell, *New Evidence That Demands a Verdict*, 12.

4. Herrick, *Case against Evangelical Christianity*, 47–62.

> "See, the days are coming—it is Yahweh who speaks—
> when I will raise a virtuous Branch for David, who will
> reign as true king and be wise, practicing honesty and
> integrity in the land." (Jer 23:5)

Finally, like many of the prophets, Jeremiah predicts a global apocalypse (Jer 45:4–5) where Yahweh will strike out against the entire earth to punish Israel's enemies. Jeremiah preached a great message on the spiritual nature of religion; it's all about love and the health of the human heart, but like his colleagues, he was a poor predictor. Yahweh's word about the future apocalypse never came about.

The Kingdom of God

Moving to the New Testament, we find that Jesus predicted that the coming of the kingdom of God was imminent within the generation of his followers, the first century (see Mark 1:15 and Matt 16:27–28). Here is what Luke quotes Jesus as saying:

> I tell you truly, there are some standing here who will not
> taste death before they see the Kingdom of God. (Luke
> 9:27)

Paul makes the same mistake (see Rom 13:11–12). In my book on evangelical Christianity, I did another study. I underlined every reference to the coming kingdom in the New Testament.[5] There were over one hundred references. Not one reference even remotely suggested there could be a delay of two thousand years. In fact, every reference suggested the kingdom was coming in the first century. Most of these statements were made by Jesus. If the New Testament is inerrant, the word of God, how could God speaking through Jesus consistently make such a mistake?

---

5. Herrick, *Case against Evangelical Christianity*, 162–66.

OLD TESTAMENT STORIES

We now turn to a different set of problems which relate to the use of the Old Testament in story creation about Jesus. The Jews did not view their sacred Scripture as a history of the people of Israel but rather as a blueprint of what God intended for the future. The Old Testament was predictive. It was seen as the word of God, which was addressed to the present as well as the past. Jews paid special attention to the big events of their history. These events were seen as pointing to a pattern of divine action which would be repeated in the future.

From an early Christian perspective, the Old Testament was seen as a book about the Messiah. Jesus was believed by his early followers to be the Messiah. As a result, the Old Testament was all about him. Using Old Testament material to create stories about Jesus was therefore seen as a legitimate practice.

A good example of this practice is the story of Jesus' triumphant entry into Jerusalem (Mark 11:1–10) on a colt, with some people spreading their coats on the road and others spreading greenery cut from their fields. This story was inspired by Zech 9:9. Read it. Mark chooses this passage in Zechariah because the king in the story is meek and gentle. He rides into Jerusalem on a colt rather than a war horse. He establishes his kingdom peacefully. The words of the crowd in Mark's story were most likely taken from Ps 118:

> Hosanna! Blessings on him who comes in the name of the Lord. (Mark 11:10)
> Blessings on him who comes in the name of Yahweh! (Ps 118:26)

This story in Mark is most likely fiction, a story created by the evangelist to make a point about Jesus, the Messiah. Because he believed the Old Testament was all about Jesus, the story in Zechariah about a king who was humble and who would bring peace to Israel must be a story about Jesus. Why do we suspect the story of Jesus' entry into Jerusalem was fictional? Remember, this was Passover—a celebration of the freeing of the Israelites from Egyptian colonial rule. Many Jews in first-century Palestine were waiting for God to repeat that miracle. The Romans were on edge, with many additional troops deployed to protect against troublemakers during the festival. There was only one road into Jerusalem. It only makes common sense to imagine Roman soldiers patrolling that road. If Jesus had in fact entered Jerusalem on a colt with an enthusiastic crowd support proclaiming him a king, the Romans would have arrested him on the spot.

This point is reinforced in Matthew's version of the story (21:1–11). According to Matthew, as Jesus enters the city, Jerusalem is in turmoil (21:10). There is no way Rome would have allowed such an entry under those conditions.

A second example comes from 2 Kgs 4:42–44. There Elisha feeds one hundred men with twenty barley loaves, with bread left over. All four Gospels report the story of Jesus feeding five thousand stranded followers with five barley loaves, with bread left over. God's work in the past was believed to predict the future. The Gospel writers also wanted to make the point that Jesus was greater than Elisha. He fed five thousand. This example will receive further support in the discussion of the miracle stories toward the end of the chapter.

A final example of the use of the Old Testament for story creation comes from Matthew's virgin birth story.[6] Rumors have persisted for centuries that Jesus' birth was not legitimate. Hints of such a possibility appear in Mark's Gospel when Jesus returns to preach his first sermon at Nazareth. The people of Nazareth were astonished when he spoke and many said, "This is the carpenter, surely, the son of Mary" (6:3). The designation "son of Mary" is a strange one in a patriarchal society where children were universally known by their father.

Bishop Spong speculates in *Biblical Literalism: A Gentile Heresy* that Matthew creates his genealogy to defend the birth of Jesus. The genealogy (Matt 1:2–16) dates back 1,800 years. Obviously,

---

6. Two further examples of this practice are seen in Luke's use of two Old Testament stories from 1 and 2 Kings to create stories about Jesus as a miracle worker. See pp. 24–25.

this genealogy was not based on historic records that did not exist, and if you compare it with Luke's genealogy (3:23–38), there are no parallels. What is interesting is the list in Matthew includes four gentile women, all with discredited sexual pasts. These four women from Jesus' line are Tamar, a prostitute for Judah; Rahab, a prostitute for the city of Jericho; Ruth, a seductress; and Bathsheba, the woman David seduced who became the mother of Solomon. By linking Jesus to these four women, Matthew suggests God can create something holy from a discredited past. The author uses the Old Testament to help make this point.

There is a related issue for us to investigate. First-century Jewish Christians and many conservative Christians today believe Jesus fulfills Jewish Scripture, that the writings in the Old Testament point to him. I was taught as a child that Jesus fulfilling Scripture proves the historicity of the Christian Bible.

In my book on evangelical Christianity, I discredit this idea. I do it by testing several New Testament claims that Jesus fulfills prophecy. It was a large research undertaking. I found there is little or no credibility to the idea. For a full discussion of my findings, you should consult my book.[7] For now, I will examine two fulfillment claims from the virgin birth story in Matthew and conclude with one pertaining to the death of Judas.

Matthew, more than any other evangelist, made claims that Old Testament passages pointed directly to Jesus. Our first example comes from Matt 2:15. In the story, God tells Joseph in a dream to take the baby Jesus to Egypt in order to escape the wrath of Herod. Remember: Herod kills all those children in Matthew's virgin birth story. Matthew claims this action fulfills Hosea 11:1: "I called my son out of Egypt." But the Hosea passage actually refers to God's liberation of the people of Israel from their captivity in Egypt. Please explain to me how the great event of Israel's escape from Egypt as described in Exodus has any relation to God telling Joseph in a dream to take his family to Egypt to escape the wrath of Herod.

---

7. Herrick, *Case Against Evangelical Christianity*, 73–98.

The second example comes from Matt 2:18. When Herod kills all the children, Matthew claims this action fulfills Jer 31:15–16. A careful reading of the Jeremiah passage indicates a problem. The children Rachel laments in Jeremiah have not been killed, but rather they are lost. They are eventually found and returned to their mothers. The two stories have few, if any, parallels.

As an aside while we are on the virgin birth story, the claim of Matthew and Luke that Jesus was born in Bethlehem is an example of prophecy creating history. Read Mic 5:2 where the prophet says the Messiah would be born in Bethlehem. There is a large scholarly consensus that Jesus was in fact born in Nazareth. Because of the belief that the Old Testament is a blueprint of what God intends for the future, Matthew and Luke created their virgin birth stories to have Jesus born in Bethlehem. I suspect Matthew and Luke knew few, if any, historical details surrounding the birth of Jesus. However, God, through the prophet Micah, predicted the Messiah would be born in Bethlehem. As a result, both Luke and Matthew invented stories to confirm Micah's prophecy. "Oh Little Town of Bethlehem," sung by millions of Christians in celebration of Jesus' birth, cements this distortion of history in the minds of most Christians.

The last example of Jesus fulfilling prophecy pertains to the death of Judas. I end with it because it is a good example of how careless and nonsensical these claims tend to be. In Matt 27:3–10, the claim is made that the death of Judas fulfills Jeremiah. The first problem is the actual reference comes from Zech 11:12–14. Compare the story of Judas' death in Matthew with the Zechariah passage. There is no relation between the two passages, with the exception of a few shared words.

Jewish sacred Scripture inspired stories about Jesus. The Old Testament was "in the heads" of the evangelists. When something about Jesus triggered their memory of an Old Testament story, they used it to fill in details from stories that came up from the oral tradition or to invent a story about Jesus that supported a claim they were making about him. As the three examples above suggest, as well the many others discussed in my book on evangelical

Christianity, the claims of prophecy fulfillment seem rather ham-fisted to me, but that undoubtedly reflects my twenty-first-century perspective.

PASSAGE PICKING

There is no better way to uncover the many contradictions in the Bible than the use of passage picking. Many scholars who write on the connection between religion and politics use passage picking to support their positions. They state a political opinion on an is-sue and find a passage in the Bible they believe supports it. The problem is the Bible has so many contradictions, you can find a passage to support any position you choose to take. This problem can be readily seen if we compare two contemporary writers in the field.

Wayne Grudem is the author of *Politics According to the Bible*. According to Grudem, God intended the Bible to give guidance in every area of life, including politics.[8] His book could have been written by a staff member of the Republican National Commit-tee or the Trump White House. Grudem finds a biblical passage to support small government, school choice, lower taxes, a strong military, greatly reduced government regulation, an out-of-control Environmental Protection Agency, and the absolute right to own a gun.

In contrast, Jim Wallis, another passage picker, comes to very different conclusions. In *God's Politics: Why the Right Gets It Wrong*, Wallis cites Christian Scripture to support nuclear disar-mament and the massive transfer of wealth to poorer nations. He supports responsible gun control legislation and policies to reduce economic inequality in the United States, as well as policies to combat racism. His politics reflect the Bernie Sanders wing of the Democratic party, with a biblical passage to support each position taken.

---

8. Gruden, *Politics According to the Bible*, 1.

Let's briefly look at the positions of the two writers on the role of government in the economy. Grudem argues the teachings of the Bible support private ownership, free market capitalism, and limited, at best, government regulation. He cites Gen 1:28 to suggest that God wants economic growth. Private property is sacred, as is seen in the seventh commandment, "You shall not steal" (Exod 20:15). Because we are created in God's image (Gen 1:27), God wants us to be like him. When we own private property, we reflect his glory.[9]

Again, by contrast, Jim Wallis points out there are several thousand passages in the Bible calling for economic justice and support for the poor.[10] He cites passages in Isaiah and Micah promoting economic justice. The psalms, according to Wallis, are all about defending the oppressed. Leviticus calls for freeing slaves, forgiving debt, and redistributing land. In the New Testament, the Beatitudes bless the poor, and Matt 25:31–41 blesses those who help the poor. The teachings of Jesus are all about economic justice and the dangers of excessive wealth accumulation. As this brief comparison suggests, the two writers find biblical passages to support the contrasting political positions they take. Sadly, the Bible, with its many contradictions, cannot be used as an ethical road map for the making of political decisions from a Christian perspective.

WORLDVIEW PROBLEMS

While we know little about the evangelists, one thing we do know is that they saw the world very differently than we do. For the evangelists, the earth was flat, with heaven as a physical place. Stars were viewed as windows through which God peeked out at us humans. Mountains put you closer to God; clouds hide the divine presence. If one was planning to sin, it was best to do it on a cloudy night when God was unable to witness it.

9. This is just the tip of the iceberg. See chapter 9 in his book for a full listing of the biblical passages supporting free market capitalism.

10. See Wallis, *God's Politics*, 209–221.

A good example of this worldview is found in Matthew's story of the transfiguration. This story takes place on a mountain where God's presence is hidden in clouds.

> He [Peter] was still speaking when suddenly a bright cloud covered them with a shadow, and from the cloud there came a voice which said, "This is my Son, the Beloved; he enjoys my favor. Listen to him." (Matt 17:5)

In addition, ancients had no idea the universe was governed by laws of nature. Instead, God held the whole thing together. History was shaped by God—the central assumption made in the Old Testament. As such, God sends or withholds rain, calms seas, brings storms, opens and closes wombs, causes crops to grow. Not surprisingly, Jews in first-century Palestine saw Israel as the center of the universe.

These Jews and early Christians also saw the world as being inhabited by tangible spirits. Demons represented Satan or the power of evil. Angels were forces supporting God. These spirit forces challenged each other. The New Testament depicts a battle between God and Satan for control of the universe. The realm between the earth and the moon was seen as the place where these spirits "hung out." A person who could command demons was seen as having divine power. There were lots of people believed to have such power, Jesus among them.

A good example of this spirit-saturated worldview is the understanding of disease, which was seen as being caused by evil forces invading the body. Ancients had no idea of the biological causes of disease. When Jesus healed disease, he was defeating the forces of evil, defeating Satan, not dealing with the biological processes we moderns associate with the cause of disease. Consider this example from Luke.

> One Sabbath day he was teaching in one of the synagogues, and a woman was there who for eighteen years had been possessed by a spirit that left her enfeebled; she was bent double and quite unable to stand upright. When Jesus saw her he called over and said, "Woman, you are rid of your infirmity," and he laid his hands on her. And

> at once she straightened up, and she glorified God. . . .
> And this woman, a daughter of Abraham whom Satan
> has held bound these eighteen years—was it not right to
> untie her bonds on the Sabbath day. (Luke 13:10–13, 16)

The question becomes, How much guidance can the Bible provide people living in the twenty-first century when we view the world so differently from our ancient first-century ancestors? As I pointed out in the section covering prediction problems, Jesus thought God would intervene to establish his kingdom within the generation of his followers. With such an expectation of an imminent intervention by God, it made some sense to surrender all of your wealth and follow Jesus. For people living in the twenty-first century and hoping to retire at age sixty-five with the expectation of a long retirement, it doesn't make much sense to surrender all of your wealth when you become a Christian.

We live in a world where 30 percent of our economy depends on international trade, where companies have offices and manufacturing plants all around the world, where employees travel and communicate daily with counterparts in distant places. Few complex, big ticket items are made solely in America. For those who live at or below the poverty level, there are government programs to provide needed support.

In contrast, first-century Palestine was a peasant economy based on subsistence agriculture and some crafts. Most goods were bartered rather than sold on the market. Tools were frequently shared among families. Most residents never ventured forth from their village during their lifetime. While the plea of Jesus for economic justice has universal relevance, many of his specific teachings on economics do not provide much help when dealing with contemporary problems. The context and the nature of the problems are worlds apart.

The teachings on nonviolence have similar problems. To begin with, it is impossible to discern what Jesus' teachings on nonviolence mean. Are the teachings on nonviolence meant to be a universal ethic or a strategy to deal with a specific first-century threat? The New Testament provides no clues as to what Jesus intended here.

Rome leveled Sephoris, a city three miles from Nazareth, a few years before Jesus was born. It's highly likely Jesus lost family members—grandparents, uncles, and aunts. It's also known that Roman soldiers were stationed in Nazareth while this slaughter was taking place. Male members of this tiny village were enslaved. Female members were forced to service Roman soldiers. These atrocities could have easily included Jesus' parents. With a vivid knowledge of this tragic chapter in the history of Nazareth, Jesus may have preached nonviolence, not as a universal ethic, but as a strategy on how best to survive Roman colonialism. God will take care of Rome. If we create loving communities, we can learn to ignore Roman oppression.

A related problem is the simple society in which Jesus lived. In living out the second commandment to love your neighbor, it was not hard to decide who your neighbor was in first-century Palestine. You knew everyone in your village. Defining the current problem of climate change in terms of neighbor need is a little more difficult because the neighbors who will be most affected by global warming have yet to be born. While Jesus' teachings inspire us to live our lives differently, there are few direct parallels between these teachings and modern societal problems.

Finally, we must deal with the miracle stories. When it comes to the miracle stories, there's a general answer and a specific one. Jesus had a reputation as a miracle worker. All four Gospels report on his miracles. Josephus, the first-century Jewish historian who wrote about this period, describes Jesus as a doer of great deeds. This piece of evidence is particularly impressive because Josephus was a nonbeliever. So, the claim that Jesus had a reputation for performing miracles is historically credible. The difficulty comes in assessing individual stories. You can't work back through the oral tradition to the time of Jesus to verify their historicity, and there are problems.

In discussing the worldview of ancient people above, we looked at the different understanding of disease. To review briefly, people in first-century Palestine believed disease was caused by Satan invading the body. Sickness was seen as punishment for sin.

> Then some people appeared, bringing him a paralytic stretched out on a bed. Seeing their faith, Jesus said to the paralytic, "Courage my child, your sins are forgiven." (Matt 9:2. See also Luke 5:20)

As previously mentioned, ancients had no idea of the biological causes of disease. When Jesus cures disease, he is attacking Satan, the power of evil. In doing so, he is bringing in the kingdom of God. The miracle stories were created, in part, to communicate that message. The fact that the kingdom of God never arrived and the power of evil remains a force in the world discredits both the theory of disease held in the ancient world and the fact that Jesus succeeded as a miracle worker in defeating it.

> At sunset all those who had friends suffering from diseases of one kind or another brought them to him, and laying his hands on each he cured them. Devils too came out of many people, howling. (Luke 4:40–41)

In addition, from Luke: "But if it is through the finger of God that I cast out devils, then know the kingdom of God has overtaken you" (11:20–21).

These healing miracles were also used by the Gospel writers to proclaim Jesus as the Messiah. Isaiah prophesied the signs that would become evident when the kingdom was here. You will know when the kingdom is here, according to Isaiah, when the blind see, the deaf hear, the lame walk, and the tongues of the dumb are untied (35:1–6). Mark reports a miracle for each sign. (See Mark 2:1–12; 7:31–37; 8:22–26.) Note again that the kingdom never arrived.

The nature miracles can also be understood in the same way. When Jesus calms the storm (Mark 6:47–52), he is ending the chaos of Satan and bringing in God's rule. Nature miracles were not unique to Jesus. Humans believed to have powers over the natural world included Apollonius, Pythagoras, Moses (Exod 14:15–24), Joshua (Josh 3:1–17), Elijah (1 Kgs 17:1), and Elisha

(2 Kgs 2:6–13). Alexander the Great parted the Pamphylian Sea, and Xerxes, the Persian king, walked on water. Julius Caesar and Augustus calmed the sea.[11] Do we believe the miracle stories about those listed above?

An additional problem relating to the historical credibility of the healing miracles is the fact that the disease was not diagnosed before Jesus healed the person. No follow-up study was done to see if the cure worked. For us to believe these stories today, such remarkable claims need solid evidence to support them.

It is also important to note that many miracle stories in the New Testament are based on Old Testament and Hellenistic models. There are two miracles in chapter 7 of Luke that are based on Old Testament stories of Elisha and Elijah. The miracle of changing water into wine in chapter 2 of John is a Dionysus-type miracle. Hellenism had a concept of the divine man. Its most important characteristic was that of miracle worker. Ancient believers craved the supernatural. Physical healing by miraculous means played an important role in every ancient religion in the Roman world.

Religious leaders were expected to perform miracles in the first century. It proved that God was working through them. Moses, Elijah, and Elisha of Old Testament fame were known as miracle workers. In first-century Palestine, Honi the Circle-Drawer, Rabbi Hanina ben Dosa, and the pagan Apollonius of Tyana were known as miracle workers. In the New Testament, the disciples of Jesus and Paul heal the sick, cast out demons, and bring people back to life. Stories about all of these people are very similar to those about Jesus. Do we believe them?

Finally, miracle stories in the four Gospels are used to make theological points, and, as a result, play an important role in the evangelist's story creation. An important theme in Luke is the historical Jesus was Israel's final prophet. Luke creates two healing miracle stories in chapter 7 to help make that point. The stories have close parallels to miracle stories about Elisha and Elijah. Compare Luke 7:1–10 with 2 Kgs 5:1–14. In the story in 2 Kings, Elisha heals the Syrian general through the intercession of a young

11. See Carter, *Jesus and the Empire of God*.

Jewish girl. In Luke, Jesus heals the slave of a gentile centurion through the intercession of Jewish elders. Luke has patterned his miracle story on a similar story about Elisha.

Continue your reading with Luke 7:11–17 and 1 Kgs 17:17–24. In the story in 1 Kings, Elijah brings back to life the son of a widow. In Luke, Jesus brings back to life the son of a widow. Both stories end with the words "and he gave him to his mother." Luke's point in this chapter is that both Elijah and Elisha are prophets, and prophets perform miracles. Jesus is also a prophet who performs miracles. The crowd witnessing the second miracle sees the connection immediately, and shouts out, "A great prophet has appeared among us" (7:17).

The writer of John uses a similar tactic to support his important theme relating to realized eschatology. Realized eschatology is the idea that the kingdom of God is here now and not some future event. This is John's explanation as to why the kingdom had not come as a promised imminent event. In John's Gospel, eternal life means to live with God. This is possible now in a Christian community. When Jesus dies, he releases his spirit called the Paraclete (7:39). The spirit of Jesus creates this Christian community, a community based on mutual love, compassion, and service to neighbor. This community is found in Christian churches. While the ideas of a second coming and a final judgment are present in John, these ideas are greatly de-emphasized. John's focus is on the present where followers of Jesus will live with God in Christian communities.

The bringing back to life of Lazarus (11:1–44) spells out this theme. It is the most amazing miracle story in the New Testament, and it is only found in John.[12] Most Christians are familiar with the story. Lazarus has been dead for four days before Jesus brings him back to life. When Jesus tells Martha, Lazarus's sister, that Lazarus will live again, Martha replies she knows he will. He will rise on the last day. This is future eschatology—the common expectation among Christians of a final judgment and a second coming in the

---

12. Please explain to me if eyewitnesses wrote each of the four Gospels how they could have missed this incredible story.

near future. No, Jesus tells her. I am the resurrection. If anyone believes in me, that person will have life now (11:25–26). This is realized eschatology—a central theme of John's Gospel. He uses a miracle story to make his point:

> I tell you most solemnly, whoever listens to my words, and believes in the one who sent me, has eternal life; without being brought to judgment he has passed from death to life. I tell you most solemnly, the hour will come—in fact it is already here—when the dead will hear the voice of the Son of God, and all who hear it will live. (John 5:24–25).

In his book *The New Testament: A Historical Introduction to Early Christian Writing*, Bart Ehrman reports an interesting story under the heading "One Remarkable Life."[13] To paraphrase the story, from the beginning his mother knew he was no ordinary person. His birth was both miraculous and accompanied by supernatural signs. He was recognized as a spiritual leader from his youth. As an adult, he went from place to place preaching a message focusing on attaining spiritual goals not material ones. He had disciples, many of whom were convinced he was the Son of God. He performed miracles: healing the sick, casting out demons, raising the dead. At the end of his life, he was placed on trial by Roman authorities for crimes against the state. His life, however, was not bound by death. Some of his followers claimed he had ascended to heaven, while others said he had appeared to them alive, that they had talked with him and touched him.

The remarkable life described in Ehrman's book is not Jesus of Nazareth but Apollonius of Tyana, a Pythagorean teacher and pagan holy man of the first century. His life and teachings are recorded in *The Life of Apollonius* by Philostratus. Let me repeat a central concern I have with the historicity of the miracle stories. Do we believe all the miracle stories coming out of the ancient world or only those pertaining to Jesus?

---

13. Ehrman, *New Testament*, 17.

But here's the biggest problem I have with the historicity of the miracle stories. They assume that God intervenes directly in human affairs to change an outcome. Ancients made that exact assumption. If that was true two thousand years ago, why did God stop intervening?

I find no evidence that God continues to act in this way. Think about the Holocaust, for example. Six million Jews prayed to the same God Christians do, asking God to intervene and save them. Instead, six million Jews lost their lives from Nazi atrocities. No God of love who acts in history would have allowed this despicable genocide to happen.

Fifteen years ago Lyn and I were returning to our home in the North Carolina mountains from Colorado. We stopped in rural Tennessee to get gas. Lyn does all the driving, bless her heart. Because I was tired of reading, I went inside to purchase a local newspaper to do the crossword puzzle.

There was an amazing story on the front page. A tornado had struck a trailer park in the small town a week before. The tornado hit a trailer where a young couple lived with their six-month-old son. The tornado sliced the trailer in half, leaving the couple untouched, asleep in bed.

When the couple awoke in the morning, they noticed, to their horror, that half of their trailer was gone, along with their son. They searched frantically for him, and, forty-five minutes into the search, they found him wedged up in a tree. The little boy smiled down on them in recognition. They rescued him and found hardly a scratch. The members of the small church they attended were convinced a miracle had taken place, that God had intervened to save the little boy's life.

On page three of the paper, I read that the same tornado struck another town five miles down the road, leaving four people dead in its wake. Does a God of love pick and choose when to intervene? Not a God I want to believe in.

Yes, there is mystery in the world. Strange things happen that are hard to explain logically. People who are prayed for survive stage-four cancer, but others die who were also prayed for.

Christians love to give God credit for all the good things that happen and are good at dismissing, ignoring, or finding excuses for things that don't work out well.

In light of all of the problems presented above, how do we explain Jesus' reputation as a miracle worker? I have struggled with this question for many years and have come to a conclusion that might make some sense. Brain research tells us that people believe what they want to believe.[14] People living in the first century desperately wanted to believe in the supernatural. Great men in the ancient world were believed to possess divine powers. The power of God was believed to work through them. They demonstrated this power by performing miracles. As a result, a biographer writing about a great man many years after his death created stories to make him into a miracle worker. The fact that he performed miracles proved his greatness.

Remember that the Gospels were written in the Hellenistic world, not the Jewish world of Palestine. The Hellenistic world had a belief in "the divine man." These figures were seen as being born through a union of god and a human being. Because of this union, they had special powers which were demonstrated in their performance of miracles. The biographers of Jesus knew little about his actual history, but they believed he had special powers given him by God like the many divine men in ancient Greece and Rome. As a result, they created stories about Jesus to paint a picture of him in this image. The only fair way to evaluate the New Testament is to examine it through the lens of a first-century worldview in which it was created. Unfortunately, that worldview makes little sense to people living in the twenty-first century.

PROBLEMS WITH BIBLICAL TEXTS

The process of producing biblical texts prior to the invention of the Gutenberg press in 1455 is a fascinating one. They were copied by hand by scribes. The early papyrus scrolls had limited space.

14. See Damasio, *Decartes' Error.*

To deal with this problem, the Gospel texts were constructed with nothing more than a string of letters. There was no separation between words, no punctuation, no use of upper case. Texts were not separated by chapter and verse.

Under such conditions, copying mistakes were easy to make. Words were omitted, lines skipped, and words were misspelled. My favorite example of a misspelled word is the Greek word for rope. Change one letter and it becomes camel. When Jesus speaks about the dangers of riches (Mark 10:23–27), is it easier for a rope or a camel to pass through the eye of a needle? A scribal spelling error could have changed the meaning of this text significantly.

The problem with making one of the mistakes described above is that the alteration is copied again and again and again. These problems have been impossible to correct because the original Gospel texts have never been found. These copy problems continued until the fifteenth century when Gutenberg solved the problem by inventing moveable type.[15]

When I was reading the New Testament in Greek in college, I was puzzled by the five or six footnotes at the bottom of each page. My professor explained that the footnotes designated variant readings. A variant reading denotes a discrepancy between texts, the fact that there are different versions of a Gospel passage in other texts that were not chosen. My professor commented that the footnotes in my Greek Bible represented only the most significant variant readings that exist. Scholars who have studied this issue estimate that the number of variant readings in the New Testament exceeds 200,000.

The last eleven verses of Mark (16:9–20), which describe the resurrection encounter between Jesus and the disciples, were almost certainly added to the Gospel text by scribes. The vast majority of New Testament scholars agree with this conclusion about the added verses. These eleven verses do not appear in the earliest manuscripts we have of Mark. The sentence structure is

---

15. The above discussion is well known within the scholarly community. For an excellent presentation of these problems see Ehrman, *Misquoting Jesus*.

more complex, and the vocabulary is not typical of the Gospel as a whole.[16]

What is going on here? Scholars suggest two possibilities. The first is that the original Mark ends with verse 8 in chapter 16. If this is the case, the disciples never meet the resurrected Jesus. Though on the surface this solution to the problem may not sound plausible, it is important to note the disciples in Mark's Gospel never understand the significance of who Jesus was. The evangelist may be emphasizing that point by not allowing the disciples to meet the resurrected Jesus. It is also possible, as the second solution to the problem suggests, that the last page of a very early manuscript was lost.

In either case, the eleven verses were added by a scribe. These verses were a human creation, certainly not a reflection of the word of God. According to these added verses, belief in Jesus Christ as your savior will allow you to pick up snakes and drink deadly poison without harm (Mark 16:18). I wonder how many unnecessary deaths resulted from a literal belief in that text.

There are significant text-related problems in the Gospel of John. The story of the adulterous woman the Pharisees wanted to stone to death (7:57–8:11) was clearly an add-on. This story does not appear in the earliest texts we have of John. In addition, the prologue (1:1–1:18) that introduces the Gospel and the appendix (chapter 21) which documents the resurrection appearance of Jesus along the shores of Lake Tiberias were added by scribes to an earlier text. Again, a majority of New Testament scholars accept as valid these text-related problems in John's Gospel.

In the first century, there were no copyright laws or a sense of ownership by the author of a work. As a result, scribes felt free to add and subtract from texts as they saw fit. In the story of Jesus' arrest in Mark (14:43–50), there is a crazy insertion of a naked man who flees from the scene (14:51–52). The insertion has no relation to anything the evangelist has written about the arrest scene. Some

16. For a full discussion of these issues see Black, *Perspectives on the Ending of Mark*.

scribe for some unknown reason inserted this scene. The Gospels are full of such insertions.

Another example of an addition to a text with considerable significance is found in 1 Cor 14:26–40, where Paul talks about prophecy. Read through the text with some care. Now read it again omitting verses 34 and 35, the anti-women verses. The passage reads seamlessly without those verses. It has been pointed out by many textual scholars the anti-women verses (34–35) were inserted by a scribe.[17]

I have argued in several places that Paul was a first-century feminist, that he had a very high view of women for a first-century man. In one of the most beautiful statements in religious literature, Paul states in Gal 3:27–27, "All are baptized in Christ, you have all clothed yourself in Christ, and there is no more distinction between Jew and Greek, slave or free, male or female."

In addition, many leaders in his churches were women. At the conclusion to Romans (16:1–16), Paul sends greetings to Phoebe, a church deacon; Prisca, a fellow worker; Tryphaena and Tryphosa, workers in the Lord; and Junia, an apostle. This evidence suggests that verses 34 and 35 are suspect and were probably inserted by a scribe to make Paul's view of women more compatible with the general culture.

The text problems described above cannot be fixed because we do not have a copy of the original manuscript written by the evangelist. The earliest texts we have of the Gospels came a hundred years or more after they were first written. Bart Ehrman poses an interesting question in *Misquoting Jesus: The Story Behind Who Changed the Bible and Why,* a pathbreaking book on this topic. Ehrman asks, What does the inerrant word of God mean as it relates to the New Testament when we have so few of the original words?

17. Ehrman, *Misquoting Jesus,* 183–86.

WILL THE REAL JESUS PLEASE STAND UP?

It's not possible. Neither history nor the biblical record can find the real Jesus of history. The quest to discover the Jesus of history began 250 years ago. Since the eighteenth century, three such scholarly quests have taken place. Each new quest has been accompanied by new historical methods and techniques, and each quest has ended in more confusion. Scholars agree that Jesus was a first-century Jew from Galilee, that his parents were named Mary and Joseph, that he taught in parables, and that he was crucified in Jerusalem. But that's it. There is no further firm evidence regarding his historical life.

The main reason for this problem is the Roman/Jewish War from 66 to 73 CE. Palestine during the time of Jesus was a Roman colony. There was widespread discontent as a result of burdensome Roman taxes and threats to Jewish culture. While the Galilee of Jesus was relatively calm during his lifetime under the rule of Herod Antipas, the situation rapidly deteriorated from 40 to 66 CE, which led to direct Roman rule to stem the chaos. In 66 CE, Jewish freedom fighters seized the Roman fortress at Masada and then proceeded to throw the Romans out of Jerusalem. Rome eventually counterattacked with sixty thousand troops, one soldier for every Jew living in the city. In 70 CE, Roman troops entered Jerusalem, burned the entire city to the ground, and destroyed the temple. Mass crucifixions ensued, with tens of thousands of Jews killed. Many others were enslaved. A few lucky ones were able to flee. Jerusalem ceased to exist as a city. It became a ghost town. The Jesus movement was forced to move from Jerusalem to the Hellenistic world.

Prior to that move, there was a well-organized Jesus movement in Jerusalem under James, Jesus' brother, that came into existence soon after the crucifixion. These followers obviously collected and wrote down stories about Jesus. Sadly, these stories were lost. If Gospels were written in Palestine before 70 CE, they have never been found. Eyewitnesses were killed. The only historical data we have from first-century Palestine concerning Jesus comes from the oral tradition, stories passed down about him by word of mouth. To make things more difficult, these stories had to make the transition from Palestine to the Hellenistic world. The first Gospel, Mark, was written forty years after his death by an author who lived outside of Palestine.

Because the Gospels differ so widely on the details of Jesus' life, ministry, and mission, scholars are all over the map on these issues. Let's spend time with some of the problems. Scholars who focus their study on the Jesus of history, the Jesus prior to the crucifixion, see him differently. Some picture him as a Jewish mystic,[18] others as a Cynic-like peasant in the tradition of Roman cynic philosophers,[19] and still others as an eschatological prophet, a prophet concerned with the "end times" of history.[20] Geza Vermes portrays Jesus as a Galilean Hasid, a Jewish holy man who heals and exorcises with speech and touch.[21] David Galston pictures him as a human being, a teacher in the wisdom tradition.[22] Others see him as a prophet in the tradition of Isaiah, Jeremiah, and Ezekiel.[23] Perhaps the most controversial view comes from Reza Aslan. In *The Zealot*, Aslan portrays Jesus as a zealous revolutionary swept up in the turmoil of first-century Palestine.[24] These differences are not insignificant and point to the real problem of achieving a consensus regarding who the Jesus of history really was.

Scholars differ on key questions that pertain to Jesus' life: Why did Jesus go to Jerusalem? Did he anticipate his death? Did he see himself as a prophet? Did he see himself as more than a prophet? What does the title "Son of Man" designate? Was there a trial? Was Jesus buried? Was the resurrection of Jesus a physical event or a vision experience?

18. Borg, *Meeting Jesus Again*.

19. Crossan, *Historical Jesus*.

20. Allison, *Historical Christ*; Ehrman, *Jesus*; Fredriksen, *Jesus of Nazareth*.

21. Vermes, *Jesus the Jew*.

22. Galston, *Embracing the Human Jesus*.

23. Herzog, *Prophet and Teacher*.

24. Aslan, *Zealot*.

Let's go back a step and look at the meaning of Jesus' death on the cross. This is a key event for many Christians. For the writer of the Gospel of John, Jesus' death was seen as an atoning sacrifice. Jesus, for John, was the perfect sacrifice, the lamb of God who takes away the sins of the world. Jesus died on the cross for our sins, which is what most Christians like to believe.

The Gospel of Luke places no such significance on Jesus' death. Luke portrays the historical Jesus as Israel's last prophet. As Jesus dies, the earth is covered in darkness, a symbol of prophetic judgment (Luke 23:44). There is no hint in Luke that the death of Jesus has anything to do with sin or an atoning sacrifice demanded by God.

My preferred explanation for the significance behind Jesus' death comes from Mark. According to Mark, the experience of innocent suffering leads one to God. The Roman centurion provides the clue. As Jesus suffers on the cross, the Roman centurion, as a witness to the event, declares, "In truth, this man was a Son of God" (Mark 15:39).

As Jesus dies in Mark's account, the veil of the temple is torn from top to bottom. Jews believed that God resided in the temple in a room called the holy of holies. Because God was regarded as so sacred, the presence of God was hidden by this veil. The only person allowed in that room was the high priest—and only once a year when he performed an atonement ritual on behalf of the people of Israel during the Yom Kippur celebration. Mark is telling us that all that changed with Jesus' death. Now, through a deep experience of the suffering surrounding Jesus' death on the cross, all people would receive access to God. The monopoly of the high priest was broken. Again, like Luke, there is no hint in Mark that Jesus' death had anything to do with sin or an atoning sacrifice.

What is one to believe? A literal reading of the Gospels presents three distinct views.

Let's look at the important question of salvation. Where is the kingdom of God located? Where will salvation take place? Stephen, the first Christian martyr, has a vision of Jesus in heaven at the right hand of God. Salvation is in heaven (Acts 7:55–56). Paul has a similar view (see Acts 9:1–9 and 1 Thess 4:13–18).

On the other hand, Jesus prays to his Father in heaven (the famous Lord's Prayer) that God's kingdom comes to earth as it is in heaven. While heaven is the model, the location is earth (Matt 6:9–10) In addition, Jesus promises his disciples they will sit on thrones to judge the twelve tribes of Israel, implying quite clearly that God's kingdom will be on earth (Luke 22:28–30).

There is a little confusion as to who will be the citizens of the kingdom: the people of Israel or all the peoples of the world. Jesus states two positions on this issue as is reported in Matthew.

> Do not make your way to Gentile territory, and do not enter any Samaritan town; go instead to the lost sheep of the House of Israel. (Matt 10:5–6; see also Matt 15:24)

> Go, therefore, make disciples of all the nations; baptize them in the name of the Father, and of the Son and of the Holy Spirit. (Matt 28:19)

Finally, there is confusion on how one gains entrance to the kingdom. Was one saved by grace—an undeserved gift from God, as reported by Paul—or did one have to earn admission by doing good works, the position of Jesus? A careful reading of the Sermon on the Mount (Matt 5–7) makes Jesus' position on works quite clear. The contrast in views between Jesus and Paul is documented in the two passages cited below:

> No; that faith is what counts, since, as we see it, a person is justified by faith and not by doing what the law tells him to do. (Rom 3:28; see also Rom 4:13–16 and 11:5–6)

> For the Son of Man is going to come in the glory of his Father with his angels, and he will reward each one according to his behavior. (Matt 16:27)

Here's the point of all this. If the Christian faith is about belief in Jesus, what is a person to believe? If one is honest about it, an objective assessment is not possible. There is no reliable historical data upon which to anchor belief. This problem does not bother many Christians, however. Why? Because they invent their own Jesus by carefully selecting the facts about him in the New Testament that suit their needs and wishes. They then ignore passages in Scripture that do not support their picture.

The fact that neither the New Testament nor history can find the real Jesus enables anyone to invent their own Jesus. This practice began in the first century with the early church. A discussion of their invention is the subject of the next chapter.

CONCLUSION

The above analysis makes one thing abundantly clear. The Christian Bible is a very human book. The idea that God inspired these sacred writings so that they come to us without error is ludicrous. The problems discussed in this chapter are plain for all to see, but I can forgive them. They are the same problems that appear in all sacred Scripture. Despite its problems, the Bible has beautiful pictures of the prophets with their passionate concern for economic and social justice. The religion of Jesus featuring a God of love and forgiveness, as well as his concern for inclusion, the practice of nonviolence, and his passionate commitment to economic and social justice, is inspiring and shines through the otherwise murky pages of the Gospels created by all the contradictions and conflicting voices within them.

There is a problem with all of this that I can't forgive, however. The contemporary church, for the most part, hides these problems from its members. The professional church leader in mainline Protestant denominations and the lay church member have totally different perspectives on the Bible. The church leader is trained in a seminary, which exposes its students to the historical-critical study of the Bible. That professional is fully aware of all the issues presented in this chapter. Yet most lay church members have a view of the Bible they learned as children. The professional church leader is afraid to challenge his or her members for fear of losing them. This dishonesty is inexcusable.[25]

I had a personal encounter with this dishonesty many years ago when I applied to be an adult Sunday school teacher in the mainline Episcopal church in our town. The minister requested that I interview for the position. He asked me to give him an idea about what I would be teaching.

Because of my fascination with the writing of the four Gospels, I told him I would begin there. I would explain why Mark was the first Gospel to be written and why it was highly unlikely it was written by an eyewitness. I would then move on to hold a class on how the authors of Matthew and Luke used Mark in writing their Gospels as well as sources of their own from the oral tradition and Q.[26]

With the mention of Q, he interrupted me. "I haven't heard mention of Q since seminary. You're bringing back a lot of good memories. But I want you to be careful. There is a difference between gently challenging and threatening."

I assured him that I was gentle, that I had received a teaching award at my university in which the chancellor praised me for dealing with controversial subjects in a gentle manner. That reassured the minister, and I got the job. The class went well, and over time we became known as the "Heretics," a label that combined the subject matter of the class with my last name. An amazing change took place, however, when I walked from my classroom to enter the church sanctuary for the service. My twenty-first-century perspective on biblical issues was replaced with the religion of my childhood. As the next chapter makes clear, the religion of my childhood is an invention of the early church.

---

25. An excellent treatment of this dishonesty is found in Good, *Dishonest Church.*

26. Q is a mysterious Gospel that has never been found. Many scholars argue that both Matthew and Luke copy from it in their Gospels. These scholars arrive at this conclusion because there are identical passages found in the two Gospels that are found nowhere else in the New Testament.

2

A Message Hijacked

THE MOST IMPORTANT REASON for moving toward a post-biblical future for the Christian faith goes back close to two thousand years. The first-century church in Palestine hijacked the message of Jesus. In doing so, it created a new religion, an invented set of beliefs that had no connection to the Jesus of history. We will examine this problem by first looking at the religion of Jesus and contrasting it with what emerged over the next hundred years following the crucifixion.

THE RELIGION OF JESUS

Beginning with the religion of Jesus, we often forget that Jesus was a Jew.[1] As a Jew, Jesus believed in one God, the creator of the universe and the giver of Torah, the Law of God. This God chose Israel from among all the nations and made a covenant with her, an agreement made with Moses on Mt. Sinai in which God promised to protect Israel in return for Israel obeying God's Law. Keeping the Law was an important priority for Jesus.

1. The analysis that follows in this chapter was first suggested to me by Geza Vermes in *Christian Beginnings*. For similar views on how Jesus became God, see Fredriksen, *From Jesus to Christ*; Ehrman, *How Jesus Became God*; and Rubenstein, *When Jesus Became God*.

> Do not imagine that I have come to abolish the Law or
> the prophets. I have come not to abolish, but to complete
> them. I tell you solemnly, till heaven and earth disappear,
> not one dot, not one little stroke, shall disappear from
> the Law until its purpose is achieved. (Matt 5:17–19)

On the other hand, it is well known that Jesus was a religious
reformer when it came to the Law. He was less interested in blind
obedience than the Law's inner meaning. You see this focus on the
inner meaning of the Law dramatically illustrated in the Sermon
on the Mount. Here is what Jesus says about the crime of murder.
He makes the same point about adultery (Matt 5:27–29):

> You have learned how it was said to our ancestors: You
> must not kill; and if anyone does kill he must answer for
> it before the court. But I say this to you: anyone who is
> angry with his brother will answer for it before the court.
> (Matt 5:21–22)

Jesus called his God *Abba*, an intimate name pointing to God
as a loving father who cared for his people. This God was quick to
show mercy and took joy in forgiveness. Read about this God in
Luke's parable of the prodigal son (Luke 15:11–32).

There was no confusion about the central focus of Jesus' message. He was sent to proclaim the good news of the kingdom. That
was his primary mission on earth.

> I must proclaim the Good News of the kingdom of God
> to the other towns too, because that is what I was sent to
> do. (Luke 4:43–44)

God is the one who brings in this kingdom. See the parable of the
secretly growing seed in Mark 4:26–29. Much of the information
about the kingdom is communicated through parables told by Jesus. This kingdom would exist on earth where Jesus would drink
wine with his disciples (Luke 22:18), and each disciple would rule
one of the tribes of Israel (Luke 22:28–30).

Where was the kingdom to be located? When Jesus gives his
instructions to his disciples for their missionary activities, the answer becomes clear.

> Do not turn your steps to pagan territory, and do not enter any Samaritan town; go rather to the lost sheep of the House of Israel. And as you go, proclaim that the kingdom is close at hand. (Matt 10:5–8)

Jesus teaches his disciples to pray for this kingdom to come. Every Christian makes the same prayer in church on Sunday. Jesus tells his disciples to pray like this.

> Our Father in heaven,
> May your name be held holy,
> Your kingdom come,
> Your will be done,
> On earth as in heaven. (Matt 6:9–10)

Note that Jesus doesn't tell them to pray for the second coming of Christ. God will bring in this kingdom and rule as he does in heaven. Love will replace political power in managing human affairs. Jesus shows people a new way to live in a community of love (see Acts 2:42–47). These events will take place in the first century. All these events will unfold within the generation of Jesus' followers. The coming of God's kingdom is imminent.

> I tell you solemnly, there are some standing here who will not taste death before they see the kingdom of God come with power. (Mark 9:1; see also Mark 1:15; Matt 4:17; Luke 9:27)

Jesus was not a systematic thinker. While it was clear that the kingdom was about the rule of God on earth, he gave few details on how that would work. As I pointed out above, the best source of information regarding the kingdom is found in the parables. The kingdom of God is like a mustard seed (Matt 13:31–32; Luke 13:18–19) that a man plants in his field. That smallest of all seeds becomes the biggest of shrubs that will serve as a shelter for birds. This kingdom involves major transformational changes which will provide its citizens with peace and security.

My favorite of these parables describing the kingdom is the one about yeast.

> The kingdom of heaven is like the yeast a woman took
> and mixed in with three measures of flour till it was leav-
> ened all through. (Matt 13:33)

God's rule is like yeast. It takes over your life and gives it a new quality. My favorite passage in the New Testament is about this new quality and the citizens that will enter the kingdom:

> You will be able to tell them by their fruits. Can people
> pick grapes from thorns, or figs from thistles? In the same
> way, a sound tree produces good fruit, but a rotten tree
> bad fruit. A sound tree cannot bear bad fruit, nor a rot-
> ten tree good fruit. Any tree that does not produce good
> fruit is cut down and thrown on the fire. I repeat, you will
> be able to tell them by their fruits. (Matt 7:16–20)

As Jesus suggests here, when God intervenes there will be a judgment. Those citizens admitted into the kingdom are the ones who bear good fruit—those who love their neighbor, who treat others justly, who give to the poor, the peacemakers of the world, those who forgive and show mercy, the generous, those willing to make the kingdom the central focus of their lives. It's all detailed in the Sermon on the Mount (Matt 5–7).

The leading members of the kingdom are the poor. "How blessed are the poor: the kingdom of God is yours" (Luke 6:20). The wealthy are not excluded, however, as we learn from the story of Zacchaeus. Zacchaeus was a senior tax collector in Jericho and a wealthy man. In meeting with Jesus, Zacchaeus promised to give half of his money to the poor and to pay back anyone he has defrauded seven times over. On hearing this Jesus proclaims, "Today salvation has come to this house" (Luke 19:1–10).

The historical Jesus was not portrayed in the Synoptic Gospels as thinking he was divine. Mark answers that question for us. When the rich man comes to ask Jesus what he must do to inherit eternal life, he begins with the words "good master." Jesus responds to him:

> Why do you call me good? No one is good but God alone.
> (Mark 10:18)

When James and John, the sons of Zebedee, come to Jesus and ask for special seats in the kingdom, Jesus makes the same point: only God can grant such a request.

> Very well, he said, you shall drink my cup, but as for the seats at my right hand and my left, these are not mine to grant; they belong to those to whom they have been allotted by my Father. (Matt 20:23)

This picture of the human Jesus of history was soon to change.[2]

THE RELIGION OF PAUL

We have little biographical information about Paul. He is thought to have been born around the same time as Jesus. He had his famous conversion experience around 37 CE. His missionary work began in 37 CE, and he died in Rome in 67 CE. He was clearly a Jew and thought by many to be a Roman citizen from Tarsus in south-central Turkey. He was obviously well-educated, as his written letters demonstrate.

Paul certainly knew about the historical Jesus because he admits to persecuting the followers of Jesus after the resurrection, and he spent time with some of the disciples on trips to Jerusalem. While traveling to Damascus (see Acts 9:1–7), he had an experience that changed his life. He was thrown to the ground, encased in light, and the voice of Jesus asked him why he was persecuting him. He later learned from the disciple Ananias that Jesus had appointed him to bring the Gospel to the Gentiles (Acts 9:15–16). This encounter with Jesus was one of deep, transforming love. God loved him despite his very troubled past. He became a new man with a renewed mind (Rom 12:2).

This transforming experience at Damascus defined his religion. The first point to make was that Jesus initiated the experience, that he, Paul, had nothing to do with it. He was totally undeserving to receive unconditional love from the man whose

---

2. For an excellent study of the religion of Jesus, see Vermes, *Authentic Gospel of Jesus*.

followers he had been persecuting. He felt that he had been saved as a person, united with a God of love he had never known before, and this great gift was something he could not have done on his own. Instead, he was saved by God's grace, an undeserved gift. As a Jew he learned from the experience that the Law had no power to do this, and thus he no longer considered obedience to the Law relevant in reconciling one to God.

The religion of Jesus, in which you performed good works to bring in God's kingdom, was replaced with faith in the person of Jesus to do for you what he had done for Paul. An important change of focus resulted. The God-centered religion of Jesus was replaced with a religion where Christ became the center.

For Paul, his Damascus experience taught him that love was the essence of Christianity, Christ living in him. The only ethical rule was to love your neighbor. If the believer was in Christ, a transforming experience followed in which the love of God took over one's personality. The believer became a new creation. Ethics came from a transformed mind. The person would then live by love for the good of others.

> Do not model yourselves on the behavior of the world around you, but let your behavior change, modeled by your new mind. (Rom 12:2)

Another important theme for Paul was the cross. Christ died for our sins. Jesus in his death bears the sins of all humanity. He enables humans through his sacrifice on the cross to become reconciled to God.

> Well then, in the first place, I taught you what I had been taught myself, namely that Christ died for our sins. (1 Cor 15:3)

This view of Jesus' death is almost certainly contradicted by the historical events of the first century. Rome could have cared less about a man chosen by God to be a sacrifice for human sin. Jesus was crucified because the temple elite were scared to death about Jesus the reformer who called into question the hypocrisy and corruption of their religious practices. The high priest and his cronies talked the Romans into believing Jesus posed a threat to their rule, that he claimed to be the king of the Jews whose mission it was to replace their rule with the rule of God.

Jesus' obedience on the cross led God to raise him up. The first man, Adam, brought sin and death into the world by his disobedience, the original sin. Human effort is unable to change this situation. Jesus is the second Adam. Because of his obedience on the cross, he is the bringer of life and salvation (Rom 5:12–16). His obedience erases the stain of Adam's sin. With this idea, Paul invented the theology of atonement, the idea that Jesus died as an atoning sacrifice for our sins.

For Paul, Jesus becomes the Messiah not in life but only when he is resurrected. Paul sees Jesus in heaven. He is the first fruits of the general resurrection. This general resurrection is imminent. Jesus will soon return and meet the faithful in the clouds and take them to heaven. Salvation is no longer for a nation, Israel, but for individuals who believe Jesus is the Christ. Those believers will have their bodies transformed and made spiritual, and in that new form they will be taken to heaven.

> At the trumpet of God, the voice of the archangel will call out the command and the Lord himself will come down from heaven: Those who have died in Christ will be the first to rise, and then those of us who are still alive will be taken up in the clouds, together with them to meet the Lord in the air. (1 Thess 4:16–18)

Paul had no interest in the Jesus of history. It was all about his experience on the Damascus road. From that experience, he proclaimed a religion of salvation by grace. This salvation is for the entire world. It no longer belongs to a nation but rather to individuals who believe that Jesus is their savior. The place for this salvation is heaven. Jesus' death on the cross is seen as an atoning sacrifice that erases Adam's original sin, which makes it possible for believers to become reconciled with God.

Paul's simple formula—that one is saved by belief in the atoning sacrifice of Jesus Christ—was immensely popular. The gift of eternal life was the selling point that would catapult Christianity to become the world's leading religion as measured by the number of adherents. We have come a long way from the Galilean prophet who called on his fellow Jews to repent their sins in preparation for the imminent arrival of God's kingdom, a kingdom on earth for the people of Israel.

THE SYNOPTIC GOSPELS

The Synoptic Gospels gave Jesus a promotion. Matthew and Luke followed Mark's lead, and the resurrected Jesus became the Son of Man. Who is this Son of Man? This figure was first described in Dan 7:13 as a transcendent, pre-existent, heavenly being. He was further developed in 1 Enoch 45–71 and 4 Ezra 13:1–53. The preexistent part means that he was with God from the beginning of time. However, while seen as a divine being, the Son of Man was not understood as God's equal, as the Son of God in traditional trinitarian Christian belief. Rather the Son of Man was God's divine agent who will come from the clouds of heaven at the end of times to judge the world and bring the righteous to heaven.

There are many titles that appear in the Gospels describing the identity of Jesus—Son of God, Son of David, Lord, prophet, rabbi, teacher, Son of Man. The Son of Man title is by far the most frequently used. It appears eighty-one times in the four Gospels. In all but two cases (Mark 8:38 and Luke 12:89), Jesus speaks as the Son of Man in the first person. It is the only title Jesus claims for himself.

The church in the first century saw the resurrected Jesus as the Son of Man. While "Son of Man" statements are often on the lips of Jesus, most New Testament scholars are convinced these statements represent the voice of the church and are not the authentic voice of the historical Jesus. The reason for this assertion is that the voice of the prophet of God's kingdom in Israel is so different from the voice of the Son of Man. The two voices could not have come from the same person. Jesus talks about the coming of God's kingdom. The Son of Man talks about the coming of Jesus as the Son of Man who will land on earth after taking off from heaven. Salvation for Jesus is on earth for the nation of Israel. Salvation for the Son of Man is for individuals in heaven. The message of Jesus is delivered by a human being from the tiny village of Nazareth. The message of the Son of Man is delivered by a divine being who resides in heaven. In remaking Jesus into the Son of Man, the church has taken the human Jesus and made him into a divine being.

There is another problem with the Son of Man as it appears in Daniel. Daniel is a work of fraud. The author claims to be a captive in Babylon in the sixth century BCE, but scholars are virtually unanimous in placing the writing of Daniel in the second century BCE. While the author wants you to think his visions are clairvoyant, expressing the word of God, he writes history instead.[3]

THE GOSPEL OF JOHN

If you read John with some degree of objectivity and attention, you will note there are no parables, no exorcisms, no messianic secret, no birth story, no temptation in the wilderness, no Sermon on the Mount, no baptism by John, no transfiguration, no Gethsemane. John's passion narrative is also considerably different from the versions in the Synoptic Gospels. It is apparent that the author of John chose differently from the oral tradition than the other evangelists. As will soon be evident, his choices led to a very different understanding of both the resurrected and the Jesus of history.

One of the central themes in John's Gospel is revelation. Jesus is the revelation of God on earth. The Gospel moves from one example to the next. The prologue to the Gospel begins, "In the beginning was the Word: the word was with God and the word was God" (1:1). Jesus is the preexistent Son of God, the divine logos, the Word. He was with God from the beginning of time.

The key statement in the prologue comes in 1:17: "The word was made flesh. He lived among us." This is incarnational theology. Jesus comes from heaven and will return there after his mission on

---

3. Ehrman, *How Jesus Became God*, 64–68.

earth is finished. John says here, and throughout his Gospel, that if you want to know what God is like, look at Jesus. God and Jesus are seen as one (John 10:30). Speaking about Abraham to a group of Jewish believers, Jesus says, "In all truth I tell you, before Abraham ever was, I am" (John 8:58). When Moses encountered God at the burning bush, he asked God for his name. God responded by revealing his name as "I am," a name Jesus assumes here (Exod 3:13–15). The Trinity comes from this Gospel.

The purpose of revelation in John was to create belief. The miracle stories were not to be kept quiet as in Mark but to be broadcast for all to hear. Their purpose was to create belief. The resurrection story had a similar purpose. The word "belief" occurs ninety-eight times in John. Its combined use in the other three Gospels is thirty-four times. This is the Gospel about belief in Jesus as the Christ. Such belief leads to salvation. As with Paul, obedience to God's Law is no longer relevant when it comes to salvation.

The ultimate miracle or proof that Jesus is the Christ is the resurrection. Those who believe it, those who believe that Jesus is their savior, that he is a divine being one with God, are saved. After his death, Jesus will return to heaven to prepare a place for these followers.

> Do not let your hearts be troubled. Trust in God still, and trust in me. There are many rooms in my Father's house; if there were not, I should have told you. I am going now to prepare a place for you, and after I have gone and prepared you a place, I will return to take you with me; so that where I am you may be too. (John 14:1–4. See also 6:40.)

As with Paul, the death of Jesus was seen as an atoning sacrifice. There was an idea in first-century Palestine that the death of a virtuous person could cause God to forgive the sins of many people and spare them punishment (See John 11:49–53). John pictures Jesus in this way—the perfect sacrifice, the lamb of God who takes away the sins of the world. Jesus dies a day earlier in John in contrast to the accounts given in the Synoptic Gospels, the day of preparation, when lambs were slaughtered for use at Passover. John changed the timing of Jesus' death to make that point.

TWO DIFFERENT RELIGIONS

The early church fathers reflected on the teachings of Paul and the four Gospels for the next two hundred years following the writing of John's Gospel. It's not surprising that some disagreements emerged about who Jesus was and his relationship to God. When Constantine became emperor of Rome, he wanted a unified Christian religion. To achieve this end, he demanded that Church bishops meet in Nicea in 323 BCE to work out their differences.

There were two main camps. One was led by Arius, a priest from Alexandria. Arius argued that we can't have two Gods. Although Jesus was like God, he was not his equal. He was obviously impressed with several statements in John claiming that Jesus' oneness with God was based on love and obedience, not substance (see John 5:19 and 5:30).

The other camp was led by Arius's bishop, Alexander, who argued that Jesus and God were of the same substance, that Jesus was fully human and fully divine. Christ, like God, was present from the beginning of time, God's equal in every way. Though most of the bishops supported Arius, Constantine supported Alexander, and that support won the day. The Trinity was the result. Jesus became fully human and fully divine, a doctrine enshrined in the Nicene Creed, the statement of church doctrine that came out of the church council.

What is most interesting to me was the process in which the creed was adopted. The Council of Nicea was not a meeting of deeply religious men who came to pray together and listen in silence for the word of God. It was instead a political brawl. Bishops were bribed to take the position of the bishop of Alexandria, and those who persisted in their dissent were beaten up by hired thugs. As a result, the hijacking of Jesus' message was cemented in stone by the most human of processes.

A new religion

We now have a new religion. The human Jesus, the prophet of God's coming kingdom, a kingdom on earth for Jews in Israel, was replaced by a divine being, God's equal, who preached a new message of salvation in heaven for true believers. The historical Jesus urged his fellow Jews to obey God's Law, to do good works, which would earn them a place in God's kingdom. The Christ of the *do good works* church changed the requirements for salvation in heaven. All that was required was belief in Jesus as your savior. The Jesus of history was crucified because, as a passionate advocate of economic and social justice, he was a clear threat to the corrupt Jewish temple elite. The Christ of the church was crucified because an angry God needed a sacrificial atonement for the original sin of humankind *conditional love* as a condition for reconciliation. The God-centered worship of Jesus became the Christ-centered worship of the church. A religion focused on ethics was changed to one focused on correct belief.

An interesting question is, How did we get there? Why this dramatic shift in the focus of the Christian religion? There are three answers to this question that readily come to mind. The first is that Jesus was a difficult Messiah for first-century Jews to understand. Jesus did not fit the model of a future king or military leader. He died on a cross.

At some point relatively soon after the crucifixion, many close followers of Jesus became convinced he remained present with them in some way. Upon reflection, they came to think of the crucified Jesus as the Son of Man who God had raised from the cross and taken to heaven. Stephen, a member of the first Christian community in Jerusalem, makes such a claim. He sees Jesus in heaven as the Son of Man sitting at the right hand of God (Acts 7:56). This began a process of reflection that continued for 250 years or more.

The second explanation comes from the outcome that followed the Jewish/Roman war from 66 to 73 CE. The Jews started it by throwing the Romans out of Jerusalem in 66 CE, but this initial victory led to devastating consequences. The Romans regrouped, counterattacking in 70 CE, when they burned Jerusalem to the ground leaving God's capital city a ghost town. The Jesus movement was centered at the temple in Jerusalem at that time. The few followers of Jesus who survived were forced to flee to places within the Hellenistic world. The Jesus movement reorganized there.

Hellenistic Jews

The four Gospels were written by Hellenistic Jews, writers who grew up in a world where great men were often thought of as being gods. It is thus understandable that these writers began to think of Jesus in these terms. In fact, there may have been some copycatting going on. Christians began raising the status of Jesus to God at the same time Romans were doing the same thing for Augustus Caesar.[4] If these Gospels had been written by Palestinian Jews who held to a strict monotheism, Jesus never would have become the God pictured in the second arm of the Trinity.

Finally, the Christian movement grew and prospered in the Hellenistic world. The first meeting places for followers of Jesus were private homes, with members coming mainly from the lower classes. That changed as the movement grew in numbers. Churches replaced private homes, and bishops replaced lay leaders. As the movement became more mainline in the second and third centuries, the organizational structure of the movement was taken over by upper-class elites. These elites were more comfortable selling a message of the savior who died to save us from our sins than the man who asked his followers to give their wealth to the poor and work to create a radically inclusive society.[5]

The key change in this regard came with the passion narrative. Let's speculate some about the events leading to the crucifixion. The Gospel of John may be the most accurate in placing Jesus in Jerusalem six months prior to the Passover celebration. During that time, it is logical to assume he taught at the temple, and his message, like the prophets, attacked the corrupt practices of the temple elite. At the time of Passover, he scattered the coins of the money changers and told the dove sellers to leave. He demanded that his father's house not be used as a market place (John

4. See Ehrman, *How Jesus Became God.*

5. Carl Krieg introduced me to the role the wealthy played in changing the teachings of Jesus. See "Story of Jesus," and "Jesus and Wealth."

2:13–16). Again, according to John, the Jewish elite decided to kill Jesus long before the Passover week (11:45–54). His teachings threatened their economic well-being, and they feared his growing popularity among the common people.

Crucifixion was a Roman punishment. What seems to have happened is that Jesus' teachings of a loving community that was inclusive with shared wealth were threatening to the established order. The temple elite had good relations with the Roman colonial administrators. Most likely Caiaphas, the chief priest at the temple, convinced Pilate that Jesus had a large following who wanted him to be king. Pilate responded by arresting Jesus, placing him on a cross in an established killing field outside the city, and leaving him there to be eaten by animals, as was the common Roman practice regarding crucifixion.

Jesus was crucified because his gentle but revolutionary ideas were threatening to the Jewish establishment. But this story changed dramatically when John wrote his version of the passion narrative. Jesus the reformer was out. Instead, he died as an atoning sacrifice for human sin. Those who believed in him as the Son of Man would be rescued and taken to heaven on the last day. Jesus the savior was a much safer figure for the church establishment than Jesus the prophetic reformer.

You see the same pattern with regard to the status of women. As I pointed out in chapter one, Jesus and Paul were first-century feminists. This situation changed under the influence of the early church. First Timothy was written between 90 and 140 CE. In this letter, the author urges Christians to pray for kings and people in high places (2:1). He then goes on to forbid women to teach or have authority over men. Why? Because men were created first, and Eve committed the first sin. Salvation for women came from having children (2:9–15). Colossians, a letter falsely attributed to Paul, commands wives to submit to their husbands (3:2). Ephesians and Titus present the same message of obedience and subjugation. Inclusion of women as equal partners in society threatened the patriarchal order championed by the wealthy elite.

It's interesting to observe how people read the Bible. Forty years ago I joined a Wednesday night Bible study class for conservative Christians to do just that. The purpose of Bible study for them was to find passages in the Bible that confirmed their beliefs. They read into the Bible what they wanted to see.

In truth, we all do that. I spend a lot of time reading thought-provoking essays on the ProgressiveChristianity.org website. These progressive Christians mostly ignore the salvation stuff and focus instead on passages promoting inclusion, economic justice, and the practice of nonviolence. They too see what they want to see.

The problem is that it is so much easier to see the picture of Jesus invented by elite members of the early church. Salvation in heaven is the dominant theme throughout the New Testament. This message created by the early church is so appealing. Eternal life in heaven is the reward for correct belief. How can you turn that down? In contrast, Jesus asks his followers to give their money to the poor before joining his movement. It's not a fair fight!

An even bigger problem is that the religion of belief that the theologians of the early church created is an ideology with no connection to the human heart. Salvation in heaven is about me, me, me. It feeds the ego rather than helping to transform it in a way that is more open to the needs of others. Jesus is worshiped as a God but not followed. His ethical teachings are not what's important. The point of religion is belief in Jesus as your personal savior. The consequences of this shift in focus will be examined next.

[handwritten margin notes: "Correct belief", "no connection with the human heart", "ME, ME, ME.", "Jesus worship."]

3

The Bankruptcy of Religion as Belief

TOWARD THE END OF his famous Sermon on the Mount, Jesus sets a standard for determining true religion. "You will be able to tell them by their fruits" (Matt 7:16–20). True religion is defined by Jesus not in terms of correct belief but in terms of actions. Does a person act from his own narrow self-interest or to benefit others? A brief review of the history of the Christian church over the last two thousand years will demonstrate a very poor record when it comes to carrying out the vision of Jesus.[1] The church as a collective entity has not been the bearer of good fruit throughout much of its history.[2]

We'll begin with what some have called the Jesus Wars, wars fought primarily among Christians in the name of the Prince of Peace over issues of religious belief. The first of these wars came about in the aftermath of the Council of Chalcedon in 451.

Early Christians had a hard time resolving the problem of Jesus' nature. Some Christians focused on divinity, arguing that Jesus had one divine nature, that he was fully divine. They were

1. Much of what follows in this chapter comes from my book, *Moving Beyond Belief*. See pp. 10–23.

2. Over the years I have consulted many books on the history of the Christian church. There are some differences between them, but on most issues they are quite similar. One of the best is MacCulloch, *Christianity*.

called Monophysites. Arians focused on a more human Jesus. The group that eventually won, Chalcedonians, joined the two natures into one person. Jesus was defined as fully human and fully divine. Each group argued their formula was absolute truth and essential for salvation. Belief in the wrong formula would send you to hell.

Monophysites   This Chalcedonian solution came about as a result of historical chance. The Monophysites, those believing in a fully divine Jesus, were the dominant group in the Roman Empire for most of the first six centuries of Christian history. Two historical accidents led to their defeat.

In 449, at the Second Council of Ephesus, the Monophysites gained a decisive advantage. A vicious doctrinal cleansing took place. As I suggested at the end of the last chapter, church councils were not quiet, dignified affairs in which bishops sat together waiting for the spirit of God to descend and tell them what to believe. Instead, they were political brawls. At Ephesus, two-nature bishops were forced to return home, armed thugs beat up dissenters, votes were influenced by bribery and threats. Council participants engaged in name-calling, slander, and intimidation.

Just as the Monophysites gained clear ascendancy, Emperor Theodosius II, a key supporter of the Monophysite position and an organizer of Ephesus, fell off his horse and died. He had no heirs. In the immediate aftermath following his death, Theodosius's sister, Pulcheria, became the power behind the throne. As a two-nature fanatic, Pulcheria organized the Council of Chalcedon, which met in 451 to put the church's stamp on the two-nature *2 nature doctrine* of fully human/fully divine. Had Theodosius not fallen from his horse, there would have been no Chalcedon. Jesus would have been forever defined as a divine being, as God on earth. His human side would have been seen as heretical.

Sadly, this did not end the dispute. The two sides fought for the next two hundred years. Because state power was weak during those days and unable to control private violence, armies loyal *The Jesus Wars* to bishops were given free reign. Tens of thousands of Christians were killed in what historian Philip Jenkins has labeled "the Jesus

Wars."[3] These Christians were fighting among themselves over issues of religious belief, all in the name of the Prince of Peace who taught them to love their enemies and pray for those who persecuted them.

This disastrous split over church doctrine weakened Christian unity and made it possible for Islam to spread into formerly Christian lands in the late seventh and early eighth centuries. A series of popes provided an answer to this problem. The first crusade was launched in 1074, the second in 1147. Both crusades were holy wars fought to stop the advance of Islam. The third crusade, launched in 1201, began as a war against Islam and was later directed against Eastern Orthodox Christians centered in Constantinople. Once again Christians were fighting over issues of religious belief. Popes promised their soldiers salvation in heaven for their participation in these wars to defend the faith. Such a promise has a creepy, modern ring to it.

Martin Luther really stirred things up when he sent his ninety-five theses to the Archbishop of Mainz on October 31, 1517. The immediate issue concerning his protest was the sale of indulgences, a practice the Catholic Church used to raise money with the promise that it would lead to the forgiveness of sin. Luther argued that only faith in Jesus Christ would lead to such forgiveness. The larger issue was over Church authority. The Roman Catholic establishment claimed that authority must be centered in the church as an institution while Luther and his followers placed authority solely in the Bible.

By 1525 large areas of Europe were in flames over these issues of belief. Luther praised the violent defense of his ideas. Fighting between Protestant and Catholic princes over these issues raged off and on for over one hundred years. The wars ended with the Peace of Westphalia in 1648 with a treaty that allowed each prince to determine the religion of his state. In the process, historians have estimated that between 25 percent and 50 percent of the

---

3. For a detailed discussion of these disastrous wars over religious belief, see Jenkins, *Jesus Wars*.

fighting over doctrine

populations of Germany and France lost their lives fighting over church doctrine.[4]

Moving to the modern period, Rwanda received her independence from Belgium on July 1, 1962. Rwanda is populated for the most part by two ethnic groups—the Hutus and the Tutsis— both of whom are Christian. Since independence, the majority Hutus have had a history of killing Tutsis. Events spiraled out of control on April 6, 1994, when President Juvenal Habyarimana's airplane was shot down. Hutus went on a rampage, and over a three-month period, eight hundred thousand Tutsis were slaughtered.[5]

The horrifying thing is that Roman Catholic and Protestant churches for the most part stood aside and allowed this genocide to unfold. It was a common occurrence for Hutus to attend church in the morning before heading out to commit their atrocities. The Hutu government had a strategy of encouraging Tutsis to gather in a church sanctuary, only to attack them there with vengeance. It was not uncommon for ten to twenty thousand Tutsis to be killed at a single church.[6]

A similar genocide involving Christian groups occurred within the former Yugoslavia. The breakup of the Soviet empire in Eastern Europe in 1991 led to a similar breakup within Yugoslavia. Ethnic nationalism led to the establishment of independent republics in Serbia, Slovenia, Croatia, Bosnia, Herzegovina, and Macedonia. This led to the Yugoslav Wars from 1991 to 2001. These wars involved a series of separate but related ethnic conflicts with causes deeply rooted in the history of the area.

The Bosnian War was an armed conflict that took place in Bosnia and Herzegovina between 1992 and 1995. To simplify greatly, the conflict was between the armies of the Republika Srpsk and the Republic of Bosnia and Herzegovina. The Serbian Srpsk Republika had citizens who were predominately Greek Orthodox

4. For a good discussion of the devastating consequences of the Thirty Years' War, see MacCulloch, *Christianity*, 644–47.

5. History.com Editors, "Rwandan Genocide," para. 1.

6. "The Rwandan Genocide," Holocaust Encyclopedia, United States Holocaust Museum, Washington, DC.

Christians. The Republic of Bosnia and Herzegovina, whose residents were Roman Catholics, was largely Croatian

Serbs and Croats have a long history of conflict in that area, with much of it resulting from their religious differences. The Bosnian war was characterized by bitter fighting, indiscriminate bombing of villages and cities, ethnic cleansing, and mass rape. These atrocities were mostly perpetrated by Serbians, but Croat and Bosnian forces were also involved. The war ended when NATO intervened in 1995 and launched airstrikes against the army of the Srpska Republika, forcing the Serbs to sue for peace.

On February 24, 2022, Russia invaded Ukraine. A few days prior to Russia's invasion, Russian President Vladimir Putin gave a dark speech in which he claimed Ukraine was an indispensable part of Russian history, culture, and spiritual heritage. Two days later Patriarch Krill, the head of the Russian Orthodox Church, blessed both Putin and the troops as they prepared to invade. He praised Putin's leadership as a miracle of God and framed the invasion as a larger metaphysical struggle against immoral Western values. This invasion, which has led to several charges of Russian war crimes, is an attack of Russian Orthodox Christians against their Orthodox brothers and sisters in Ukraine.[7] Christian nationalism is unfortunately a widespread problem that infects congregations the world over.

As I was working on making corrections to a first draft of this book, Hamas executed a brutal attack against Israel on October 7, 2023. This current crisis in the Middle East illustrates well the problems related to religious belief and violence which in this case involves Jews, Muslims, and Christians. I'm going to take you on a tour of Jerusalem that Lyn and I took several years ago on a trip to the Holy Land because it not only points out how mythological religious beliefs can lead to violence, but it also shows how these beliefs are perpetuated.

7. Thames, "Putin Is After More Than Land." In all fairness, as the brutality of Russia's invasion became more apparent, 280 Orthodox priests issued a statement condemning the war. It is important to note, however, that these priests represent only a small minority of priests within the Russian Orthodox Church.

In Gen 17:1–8, we learn that God got into the real estate business and gave the land of Israel to the Jewish people. I learned some interesting specifics about this gift from our tour guide. On our visit to the Temple Mount in the old city of Jerusalem, our guide pointed out the sites where God formed Adam from the dust of the ground and where Abraham prepared to sacrifice Isaac. I wondered where the site of Eve's first sin, which gave birth to the toxic myth of original sin, was located, but I was a good boy and never asked that question. I also remained silent when our guide told us that it was within the sacred grounds of the Temple Mount where God declared Jerusalem to be the eternal capital of Israel. I was wondering if God made such declarations and, if he did, why it took so long for him to deliver on his promise. From the end of Solomon's rule in the tenth century BCE until 1967, close to three thousand years, Israel has controlled an undivided Jerusalem for less than two hundred years.

We were next led to the Dome of the Rock and the Al-Aqsa Mosque, the third holiest site in the Muslim world. While we were not allowed to enter either site, we learned all about them. Muslims refer to the Temple Mount as Haram esh-Sharif or the Noble Sanctuary. According to Muslim tradition, Muhammad embarked on his famous night journey on the back of Buraq, a winged horse, sometime around 621 CE. When he landed in Jerusalem at the Temple Mount, he led Abraham, Moses, and Jesus in prayer. He then took off again and flew with the angel Gabriel to heaven, where he met with God, who he was able to convince to reduce required Muslim prayer from fifty times a day to five. Following the meeting, he returned to earth. This trip to heaven proved to Muslims that Muhammad had a unique status among all of God's prophets.

Our last stop was the Church of the Holy Sepulchre, the holiest site for Christians in the world. Two sites in particular are revered: the chapel that marks where Jesus was crucified and the chapel commemorating where he was buried and from where the resurrection took place. In sum, it was an interesting tour from which I learned that many years ago God was in the real estate business, that prophets can fly, and that two thousand years ago a man physically rose from the dead. It was never explained where that resurrected body ended up. I guess most would answer "heaven," wherever that may be.

The problem with sacred beliefs is that they become firmly embedded in the identities of those who hold them, which makes compromise on disagreements almost impossible to achieve. The result is distrust, hatred, and war.

How do such dangerous ideas persist over time? I got an insight into this problem following our tour of the old city in Jerusalem. After visiting the Church of the Holy Sepulchre, we were taken to lunch at a hotel in the new section of the city. That gave me a chance to corner the guide in private. I asked him if he was familiar with what many historians say about Roman policy toward crucifixions. Killing fields were set up outside of a city with crosses already in place. These fields were surrounded by Roman troops whose mission was to prevent family members from removing a dead body from a cross for burial. These bodies were left on crosses for animals to devour. The policy was designed to make crucifixions so horrible they would serve as a deterrent for potential political troublemakers. This policy made it likely Jesus was crucified outside of the city without burial, thus negating the story we learned at the Church of the Holy Sepulchre.

"Yes, I am familiar with that history," the guide responded, "and I'm glad you didn't raise these issues during the tour. Christians on tour want confirmation of New Testament claims. My tip jar would be empty if I suggested it was possible the body of Jesus was left to be consumed by animals."

To review briefly, the wars described above with the exception of the last example were conducted by Christians most often violently disagreeing over matters of church doctrine. In many cases, the participants believed they were fighting to honor the Prince of Peace whom they claimed was the central focus of their lives. I guess it is fair to say that actions speak louder than words. The Prince of Peace had little influence over hearts taken over by religious ideology.

Not long after the Hamas's terrorist attack on October 7, significant increases in anti-Semitic incidences were reported within the United Sates and throughout the world. Again, the scourge of anti-Semitism has biblical origins. The problem began with the evangelists spinning the passion narrative in such a way as to make "the Jews" responsible for the death of Jesus. The goal was to escape Roman persecution by convincing Roman authorities that Christians were harmless, that Pilate was not responsible for the death of Jesus, that Rome had nothing to fear from this new religion. Read the story of Jesus before Pilate in John 18:28—19:16. It didn't matter that crucifixion was a Roman punishment, that if the Jews had wanted to kill Jesus, stoning was their method. The Bible puts all the blame on "the Jews" for killing Jesus.

James Carroll in *Constantine's Sword* makes a convincing case that this belief has been responsible for two thousand years of anti-Semitism.[8] A brief overview of European history is informative. The first crusade (1096) was directed against both Muslims and Jews. The cry went out that the Jews had crucified Christ, which led to their being threatened with conversion or death.

It became a common practice for European Christians to blame Jews for all the tragic events that occurred in their lives. The Black Plague (1348–51) took the lives of between twenty and twenty-five million people. Jews were accused of causing it, which led to thousands being killed in revenge. Roman Catholics blamed the Jews for the Reformation. Both Catholics and Protestants blamed the Jews for the revolutions in Europe of 1830, 1848, and 1871.

The aftermath of the Black Plague led to hysterical anti-Semitism in Spain. In 1391, Jews were ordered to convert to Christianity or face the death penalty. This harsh discrimination was institutionalized in 1478, when King Ferdinand and Queen Isabella established the Spanish Inquisition. This religious tribunal was designed to enforce Catholic orthodoxy. Organizers were especially suspicious of the forced conversions of Muslims and Jews. Were the conversions for real or merely faked to avoid punishment?

8. See Carroll, *Constantine's Sword*.

Many converts were accused of being dangerous heretics. Over the three hundred years of the tribunal's history, 150,000 people were prosecuted and between 3,000 and 5,000 executed.[9] The religious frenzy led to mass expulsions of Jews and Muslims from Spain.

The Dreyfus Affair showed that anti-Semitism existed just below the surface in French society. An army officer and French patriot named Alfred Dreyfus, who also happened to be Jewish, was arrested and charged with spying for the Germans. He was convicted on these bogus charges in December 1894 and sent to prison. The charges of a Jew spying for the Germans led to a massive explosion of anti-Semitism in France.

One of the biggest anti-Semites in Europe was Martin Luther. For that reason, Hitler loved him. It is interesting that Pius XII, the Pope during the Nazi period, strongly condemned communism but remained silent in face of Nazi atrocities. When Hitler demanded that German church leaders sign loyalty oaths and accept his racial policies, the vast majority of German clerics went along in silence. The one prominent exception was Dietrich Bonhoeffer. Bonhoeffer was quick to point out that silence in the face of evil is evil itself, to not act is to act. Bonhoeffer lost his life fighting the anti-Jewish policy of the Nazis.[10]

The Christian church has a long, sad history of remaining silent in the face of discrimination. Churches in the Southern United States have long supported slavery even after the Civil War. Martin Luther King expected white churches in the North to be his biggest supporters. Most remained silent. The Dutch Reformed Church in South Africa has a long history in support of apartheid, the policy to keep black South Africans as second-class citizens. Such Christians believe in an ideology but have never known God's love in a deep, experiential sense. Such love naturally reaches out to those who are different.

Moving from history to a problem which has only become manifest in modern times, there is no greater long-term threat to the health of our planet than human-induced climate change. The

9. Carroll, *Constantine's Sword*, 357.

10. Metaxis, *Bonhoeffer*.

place to begin is with the science that explains the problem. There is a broad consensus among scientists that global warming is occurring because of human activity. The basic science is simple to understand. The burning of fossil fuels has increased the level of carbon dioxide in the atmosphere by 40 percent since the beginning of the industrial age. This carbon dioxide acts like a blanket by refusing to allow heat to escape from the atmosphere. The result is global temperature rise. During the twentieth century global surface temperatures have increased by 1.33 degrees Fahrenheit. Computer models suggest that by 2100, the global surface temperature will rise an additional 2 degrees F at minimum with a maximum possible gain of 11.5 degrees F.[11]

Global warming is causing glaciers to melt, leading sea levels around the world to rise. This increased heat adds moisture to the atmosphere and increases the energy in the climate system which incites extreme weather. Increased levels of carbon dioxide have also found their way into the oceans, which changes the chemistry of the water, thus posing a significant long-term threat to several species of aquatic life. Significant expenditures to contain this global scourge will now pay dividends for the future because out-of-control global warming will have enormous negative economic consequences.

As I suggest above, the consensus on these conclusions is virtually unanimous within the scientific community. Opinion polls tell us that people around the world are largely in agreement with the scientists. The picture in the United States is not quite so clear, however. Conservative Christians reject these scientific conclusions by large majorities.

Ignoring empirical scientific evidence, climate change deniers argue that only God can cause global temperatures to rise. If the planet is warming, humans have nothing to do with it. Senator James Inhofe (R-Oklahoma), the former chair of the Senate Environment and Public Works Committee, holds that view. According to Representative Paul Brown (R-Georgia), "God's word is

11. Bushby, "Why Climate Change Matters More Than Anything Else," 49–57.

true, but evolution, embryology, and the Big Bang Theory are lies straight from the pit of Hell."[12]

These men believe the world was created by God in six days and is 9,000 years old. The vast majority of evangelical Christians believe in the literal version of the two creation stories in Genesis. A similar number attribute the increased intensity of storms and flooding as evidence of the biblical end times. Their bedrock commitment to the literal truth of Scripture prevents them from seeing, as I pointed out in chapter 1, that in fact there are two stories of creation in the first three chapters of Genesis, with no common elements between them.

As I listened to the political debate pertaining to the Congressional elections in November of 2018, the climate change issue was rarely discussed. The self-centeredness surrounding this issue can be seen in the growing NIMBY ("not in my backyard") movement that is sweeping the nation. The land mass of the United States covers 2.9 million square miles. To take care of all of our country's electricity needs from renewable sources will only require 10,424 square miles of territory—one-third of one percent of the total land mass. It is also clear that wind and solar are now cheaper on a per megawatt hour cost than any other source of electricity. Despite these very favorable factors, in 2023 nearly as many counties passed legislation blocking new solar farms than those that allowed them. In 2022, more counties prevented wind farms from being developed in their counties than allowed them.[13]

You can't be in love with God without being in love with the created universe. Climate change threatens the health of God's creation as well as the quality of life of our children and grandchildren. The real danger is that there is no forgiveness with this issue. Greenhouse gases emitted into the atmosphere today will remain there for thousands of years. Christians need to stand up and join together in demanding a responsible solution to this problem. God is tugging at us to do so. There really is a better way

12. Flannery and Werline, *Bible in Political Debate*, 61.

13. Smith, "Why Plug Power, Sun Power, and Brookfield Renewable Stocks All Dropped Today."

to provide energy to fuel modern economies than a heavy reliance on fossil fuels.

The other problem that threatens the planet with destruction is the prospect of nuclear war. During the Cold War years, the United States and the Soviet Union built nuclear bombs. By 1986, the US arsenal included twenty-three thousand such bombs, with the Soviet arsenal reaching forty-thousand. Each of these bombs was, at minimum, several times more powerful than the nuclear bomb that destroyed Hiroshima in 1945. The yield of some of the larger bombs was one thousand times more powerful than the ones used at the end of World War II. The national security policies of the two states were insane. An all-out war between the two countries would have ended human life on the planet. And we came so close!

I don't think it's necessary to have a detailed discussion of the threat posed to the planet by the nuclear weapons scourge. Most readers have thought and worried about this problem from time to time. What concerns me is that Christians for the most part have remained silent on the issue. They are more concerned with earning a living, planning their next vacation, or rooting for their favorite sports team. They sense no responsibility for this grave threat to the beauty of God's creation. They can't see beyond their own personal needs because their religion of belief does not connect to their heart. A healthy heart would feel compassion and care deeply about the loss of life and the terrible destruction that would result from a nuclear war.

Sadly, the contemporary political scene in America demonstrates beyond doubt the bankruptcy of a religion of belief. Economic disparity between the top 10 percent of the population and the rest of us has never been greater. White Christian nationalists, a significant group within the evangelical movement, have consistently responded with a lack of concern for their neighbor. They've sponsored legislation to restrict minority voting, have worked to turn the clock back on LGBTQ rights, and called for the passage of xenophobic and inhuman immigration laws.

Nothing supports the bankruptcy of the religious beliefs of many evangelical Christians than their overwhelming support of former President Trump's reelection bid. Over the last several months Trump has indirectly praised the violent assault on Nancy Pelosi's husband, accused Joint Chief of Staff Chairman General Mark Milley of treason and suggested he be executed, and has endorsed the police shooting of suspected shoplifters. His campaign speeches have focused on hate for immigrant groups and other minorities, revenge against his political opponents, and personal grievance. He is currently facing ninety-one indictments in four courts. Yet the political leaders in his party, most of whom claim to go to church, have continued to support him or have otherwise remained silent. The vast majority of his evangelical base remains committed to his candidacy.

"By their fruits you will know them." The problems outlined in this chapter suggest to me that many Christians need to rethink their religion if they want to be followers of Jesus.

4

Human vs. Divine Love

FOR THE LAST TWO thousand years, the Bible has been the anchor for the Christian faith. Sadly, the findings of this book have demonstrated that the Bible as anchor has lost its footing. If Jesus is the founder of the faith, neither the Bible nor history can securely locate him. The result is that every Christian creates their own Jesus. The religion that most Christians buy into is an artificial invention of the early church. This religion is composed of several related beliefs that were drafted into final form in the fourth century by a group of politically driven bishops seeking doctrinal unity. The problem is that more and more people in the twenty-first century find those beliefs unbelievable. As a result, the Christian faith is losing adherents especially in the developed world in significant numbers. The time has come to consider new approaches to anchor the faith.

To answer the question of what a post-biblical Christian faith might look like, we need to begin with some God talk. I have given one sermon in my life, and you will soon see why I quit while I was ahead. I was a religion major in college, and at the beginning of my sophomore year, my academic advisor suggested I join the Denison deputations team. This team was a group of students who conducted services for small Baptist churches in Ohio on the first Sunday of each month.

As a new member of the team, I was spared sermon duty for several weeks, but my turn eventually came due, and I was panic-stricken about what to speak about. Thankfully, *Time* magazine came to my rescue with the publication of its famous "Is God Dead?" issue in April of 1966. I remember the cover. The background was dark black with the title "Is God Dead?" in deep red. It was stark.

On a Sunday in early May, I flashed this cover before a congregation of seventy-five Baptists, and I had their attention. The minister sitting in the front row off to the left was shooting daggers at me. Most of the congregation stared up at me in horror and disbelief.

I proceeded to proclaim that the Father in heaven who sits on a throne and counts sin is dead, and that it was time to bury him. I went on to bury some additional theistic images that made little sense to me before proclaiming Paul Tillich's God, understood as the ground of all being, alive and well. We were studying Tillich in a theology class I was taking at the time. As I tried to explain what Tillich meant by this image, I looked out at the congregation. Eyes glaring at me in horror were now shut, with many asleep.

After reflecting on the issue for more than fifty years, I think I can expand on Tillich. Let's begin with a premise many accept but seem to ignore when asked to speak about their religion. The phenomenon of God is a mystery that can't be known or defined in any rational sense. Any image one creates is like the blind men touching the elephant. In this ancient parable, several blind men come across an elephant, an animal they had never encountered before, touch one part, and describe the animal based on that one part. It's not surprising they come up with different images describing the elephant, all of which are inaccurate. Images created to describe God have the same problem.

Unfortunately for Christians who want black-and-white answers, God can only be encountered, never known or defined. It's silly trying to create images of what is essential mystery, even when those images are based on profound theological thinking. True religion, in all its many iterations, is about one thing—a heart overflowing with a love whose source is an encounter of divine energy flooding one's awareness.

Over the years I have had several encounters of deep love while spending time in nature. The encounters have come by surprise. They could not be planned or timed. I remember experiencing deep peace one afternoon, sitting on the bank of a river watching the water flow by. My awareness was flooded with a loving energy as I stared at a doe with her two fawns grazing in a meadow not far from the home of my son and his wife in Lebanon, New Hampshire. I sensed wonder and deep awe one night as I gazed at the stars and thought about the magnificent universe we all share.

There have been other encounters with similar results. I make an effort to spend time in nature. The experiences I have had there have two things in common. They were short-lived, and they came with a message. With regard to message, I did not learn that Jesus died for my sins or that he rose from the dead in three days. Instead, I sensed that life is good, the world is beautiful, that love is real. I experienced a reality so much greater than myself. For a brief moment, I was taken to another place.

The experiences helped me to think differently about myself and the world where I live. I felt connected to something so much greater than myself. In addition, the experiences created for me a profound reverence for life. I came to understand that we are tenants on this earth, not owners. The experiences were truly humbling.

Here's what seems to be happening here. Humans are bombarded by sensations from the surroundings around us that need to be organized so that we can make sense out of a world that would otherwise overwhelm us. The brain is our organizing tool. It creates structures of interpretation that act to filter new experience, which results in the creation of our own little world. On occasion moments occur that penetrate these structures of interpretation, which allows transcendent experience into our awareness. Unfortunately, these experiences are fleeting, and we quickly return to awareness governed by the structures of the world we have created.[1]

1. Krieg, "Birth and Death of the Church in the First Century."

These fleeting experiences are examples of divine love. Let me cite two additional examples. Imagine a mother in childbirth. The baby is born, and the doctor hands the baby for the mother to hold. Most likely, love floods her awareness. The world looks beautiful and good. As she enables the tiny hand of her child to grab her finger, she experiences a deep sense of awe and wonder. Holding her baby for the first time has broken down her defenses, which has allowed divine love to take over her awareness and transform her.

My second example is a strange one, given the major themes of this book. I have an Episcopalian friend who holds traditional Christian beliefs. He has often reported to me that he was overwhelmed, brought to tears, his heart soaring as he kneeled at the communion rail. He saw himself as a sinner and believed Jesus died so that his sins could be forgiven. Reflecting on Jesus' awesome sacrifice on his behalf broke down his defenses and divine love flooded his awareness. He claimed that the ritual of Holy Communion transformed him as a person, and as one who knew him well I believed him. Mythological beliefs from my perspective were able to open his awareness in a way that allowed divine love to surge into his conscious awareness and take him to a new place.

Human love works differently. Think of the warmth around the Thanksgiving table and the love and gratitude you feel for the members of your family. Imagine your best friend coming to you in tears with the news that her husband was leaving her. You attend a basketball game, and the next thing you know, your son sinks a three-pointer. Your heart swells with pride and affection.

The examples of love described above fill your heart, but they do not take you to another place. They most likely will not leave you with a sense that life is beautiful and good. You will not sense that you are part of a much larger reality. The experience will not fill you with awe and wonder. You will not feel called to lead a new life in the service of others. The organizing structures created by your brain have not been weakened in a way that allows divine love to enter your awareness. Though special, these experiences of human love are part of life as usual and derived from biological processes within.

Matthew Fox writes about divine love as a spiritual energy flooding human awareness in his profiles of the great Christian mystics—Meister Eckhart, Hildegard of Bingen, Julian of Norwich, and Mechthild of Magdeburg are among those he features.[2] One of the interesting things about them is that they paid little attention to the Bible or Christian belief. Their goal was to encounter the love of God through deep immersion in nature. From these encounters they learned compassion for others, a deep commitment to economic justice, and a passion for reconciling enemies and the practice of nonviolence. The examples of these warriors for God offer an intriguing model for us to follow.

In addition to deep immersion in nature, meditation is a way to connect with divine love. While not an expert on different meditative techniques, I have had success with a simple meditation on gratitude. Thanking God in a peaceful setting for my many blessings has often left me with a full heart and transformed mind.[3] I also practice mindful meditation as a way of dealing with my psychological junk. Understanding the source of my grievances, fears, jealousies, ambition, and other petty concerns weakens their control over my conscious awareness, makes me less self-absorbed, and weakens my defenses, which allows me to become more open to encounters of divine love.[4]

As I have indicated above, my experiences with divine love have been through brief encounters. From these experiences, I have sensed a world of goodness, beauty, and love. This world is so much larger than the narrow world of my self-interested awareness. However, because the encounters with this realm are brief, I don't naturally flow there on a permanent basis. These encounters define what is good. They help me to see and understand the needs of others, but I have to decide to act to honor the experience in a way that goes beyond my narrow self-interests. To become a

2. Fox, *Christian Mystics.*

3. See Emmons, *Thanks!*, for a wonderful book documenting the healing power of meditations on gratitude.

4. For a discussion of the many advantages of mindful meditation see my book *Moving Beyond Belief,* 29–30.

follower of Jesus, you must have a real sense of divine love in your life, and then you need to make a decision to organize your life around the world that is revealed in the encounter. Living the love behind Jesus' teachings is a challenge requiring dedicated effort.

If God is all about an encounter of goodness and love, if all true religion is about a heart overflowing with divine love, what would a post-biblical Christian future look like? To begin with, Jesus would remain an inspirational role model. He shows us what can be done if we make the decision to organize our lives around what we encounter in God's world.

We would honor the Bible for giving us a picture of a beautiful man who dedicated his life to serving his neighbor and honoring his God by working to bring in his kingdom. As a result, rather than trash the Bible, we would remove it from the pulpit and place it in the church library to serve as a reference book for this wonderful man whose teachings we continue to hold in our hearts.

The liturgy of the new church will focus exclusively on helping its members encounter deep love in their daily living. No mention will be made of sin or salvation in heaven. Church music must be carefully chosen to take congregants to another place. Lyrics reflecting traditional biblical belief will be purged and replaced by songs that praise economic and social justice, peace and reconciliation, love and inclusion. The service should also honor great leaders from all spiritual traditions in addition to Jesus. Classes on meditation will replace Bible study. A performance of the universe story will replace the Christmas pageant celebrating Jesus' virgin birth.[5] Much experimentation will be required, with the clear goal in mind of bringing the presence of God into the service.[6]

5. The universe story pictures the process of creation as one of billions of years of creative transformation. Everything had to work perfectly from the Big Bang fourteen billion years ago for human life to have emerged on our precious planet. The universe and human life were the result of a mysterious self-organizing mechanism rather than a random mechanical one. The story creates a sense of awe and wonder, which opens one to an encounter of divine love. See Swimme, *Universe Story*.

6. For church groups interested in experimenting with new liturgy, check out the ProgressiveChristianity.org website. Experimental liturgy is an

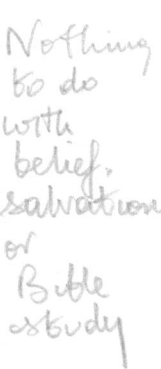

Nothing to do with belief, salvation or Bible study

One important role for the church in this post-biblical future will be to bring God's love into the world. It will have nothing to do with belief, salvation in heaven, or Bible study. The goal would be to create communities of love, to bring love into the world where there is hate, to build people up, to help members lead lives of meaning and purpose.[7] Teaching meditation and providing counseling services will help in this regard. Creating a community that shares, creates trust, fights loneliness, provides space for the healing of wounds, helps in nurturing self-acceptance within a community that is inclusive, a community that celebrates awe, wonder, joy, and gratitude, will help to breakdown defenses and allow members to become more open to encounters of divine love. When you really think about it, this focus on love represents what has always been at the center of the Christian faith.

These loving communities would also serve as a buffer against the spiritual challenges posed by modern life—the noise, the hatred spewed on social media, the problem of finding meaningful work in the age of artificial intelligence, economic inequality created by a predatory capitalist economy, the superficiality of an entertainment-crazed society, and there are others. The new church will need to anchor its members in a caring community that provides a clear contrast to the modern world, a church that promotes a culture of love to counteract forces in modern society that feed a culture of hate.

The Dalai Lama has long argued that modern life in the developed world is full of anxiety, addiction, depression, isolation, worry, and mental exhaustion. A person living under such psychological constraints will have great difficulty loving his neighbor. If that is Jesus' call to us, it is incumbent of the church to minister to these needs.

---

important focus of their work. They have done really impressive work developing a children's curriculum called "A Joyful Path." This curriculum is nature-centered, with a focus on joy, compassion, and the teachings of Jesus.

7. The Rev. Gretta Vosper is a United Church of Canada minister who has created a church along these lines. For a detailed discussion of the emerging new church, see her *With or Without God.*

The need for a reformed church was dramatically illustrated by a recent study conducted by three professors from Allegheny College involving 1,500 respondents. The study found large numbers of Americans willing to support leaders who would violate democratic principles. These citizens expressed support for strong leaders who would take uncompromising, decisive action. Many respondents were willing to bend election rules in order for their party to win. They expressed a desire for leaders who would crack down on groups they saw as undermining their values or position in society. It was seen by many as legitimate to suspend certain provisions in the Constitution to get things done. Such views were held by one-third of the Democratic respondents and 50 percent of Republican respondents.[8]

The professors concluded that these views were driven by the overwhelming need for protection among those who were willing to violate democratic norms. This study reflects the general angst that many feel concerning the direction of modern society. People increasingly experience the scary effects of climate change in their daily lives. Many worry about the effect that artificial intelligence will have on their professional lives. For perhaps the first time in American history, parents worry that their children will not live as well as they have. People work hard so they can consume, but many are painfully aware that there must be more to life. Modern life is lonely, intensely competitive, with a toxic political atmosphere and social media platforms that magnify these negative trends.

This general angst, coupled with a growing loss of meaning and purpose, could not be more timely for the future of the Christian church. These broken individuals need to belong to a loving community that would help them rebuild self-esteem and provide a new sense of meaning and purpose. Churches centered around biblical belief for the purpose of gaining salvation in heaven won't serve these needs. People are looking for a better life in this world not some future life in a place that has become increasingly difficult to envision.

8. Williams, Bloeser, and Harward, "Large Numbers of Americans Want Strong, Rough, Anti-democratic Leaders."

The new church will need to be open to the wisdom of all

Nature the great religious traditions. One of the conclusions that can be drawn from this study is that nature, God's world, is a much better source of revelation than the Christian Scriptures. With this in mind, Taoism would be an important tradition for study.

The goal of Lao Tzu's *Tao Te Ching* is to help people live wisely, to help them find personal balance by tuning into the cycles of nature. By breaking away from the frantic rhythms that drive the material world and tuning into the patterns and rhythms of nature, we can bring peace to our lives. The Tao teaches that you can't love others or hear the gentle voice of goodness and love pulsating through the universe unless you are healthy inside.[9] This teaching echoes the functions described above for the church of a post-biblical future.

There is statistical evidence to support immersion in nature as a spiritual practice that brings health and wellbeing. The Fetzer Institute released a study in the fall of 2022 entitled "What Does Spirituality Mean to Us?: A Study of Spirituality in the United States Since Covid." The study was conducted by the National Opinion Research Center at the University of Chicago. They interviewed 3,651 Americans eighteen years and older. The study found the most common spiritual practices engaged by the respondents were prayer, art, and time spent in nature. Seven out of ten people interviewed said that spending time in nature gave them a sense of peace and hope for the future.[10]

Finally, the new church must encourage its members to become followers of Jesus. Encountering divine love in brief experiences points to the way of Jesus. The church must then help its members live those teachings. Promoting charities like local food banks, women's shelters to protect against domestic violence, housing for the homeless, and providing loans to help those in financial

politics trouble is a start. But participation in politics can't be avoided. The

---

9. See Dreher, *Tao of Inner Peace*. This book not only provides an excellent introduction to Taoist philosophy, but it also offers a wide variety of spiritual practices to help the seeker achieve the goal of inner peace.

10. "What Does Spirituality Mean to Us?"

Christian right has demonstrated that it can be done with impressive results. While the church should avoid close association with one of the political parties, to implement the teachings of Jesus it should work to help achieve responsible gun control, the reduction of military spending, as well as the promotion of economic and social justice. It needs to promote policies to solve the climate crisis, treaties to end the scourge of nuclear weapons, and laws to protect the LGBTQ community.

I am one of those people who believe truth wins out in the end. We see that happening today with the significant decline in the number of Christians holding traditional beliefs. The findings of modern science and biblical scholarship have destroyed the fairy tale Jesus invented by the early church. Yes, the New Testament contains many inspiring stories. It is also true that scholars have done much good work in finding ways to make these ancient myths meaningful for modern adherents to the Christian faith. The problem, however, is the big picture. That picture is all about salvation in heaven and Jesus dying for my sins. It's a picture that the vast majority of Christians cling to, and it's a picture that has no historical validity. It is an invented religion. These Christians worship Jesus as a God but are unable to follow him, to live the love called for in his teachings. Why? Because their religion is based on ideological belief which has no connection to the heart. The only hope for the future of the Christian church is to come up with inspiring stories based on historical truth and to create a religion centered around a heart that overflows with divine love. As I have said several times in this essay, the encounter of love that is abundant and overflowing is the core of all religious truth.

A question many may have been asking as they read through these pages is, Why remain a Christian? If the Bible no longer anchors the Christian religion, what is left? There are two answers to this question.

The first is that Jesus created a model for the new church of the twenty-first century. First-century Palestine was a scary place for the vast majority of Jews living there. Roman colonialism was oppressive. Based almost certainly on Jesus' instructions, his followers created a loving community in Jerusalem following the crucifixion, centered around shared wealth and fostering loving relationships among members so that Roman oppression could be ignored. See Acts 4:32–34.

The second reason for remaining a Christian is that Jesus points out the way of true religion. The clearest presentation of the way of Jesus is found in the Didache, a church manual that most scholars date to the first century. It's a manual that reveals how Jewish Christians saw themselves and how they presented their religion to potential gentile converts. It contains three sections. The first deals with Christian ethics, the second with certain rituals such as baptism and the Eucharist, and the third involves church organization.

The first section is the relevant one here. It points out the two ways, the way of life and the way of death. The way of life requires you to love God and your neighbor as yourself. It then summarizes several teachings from the Sermon on the Mount relating to sharing wealth and reconciling with your enemies. These teachings are followed by several instructions relating to personal morality— prohibitions against murder, adultery, theft, perjury, hate, narcissism are among them. The Jesus of the Didache is pictured as God's servant. It never identifies him as a divine being.[11]

The point is that the way of Jesus is to act in a manner that reflects the love of God that fills your heart. The Didache does not tell the followers of Jesus to believe in him as a salvation figure but rather to act in ways that express God's love. Understood in this way, the religion of Jesus is the answer to solving many of the problems that threaten modern life.

The loving energy that comes from an intense experience of the beauty of the natural world will cause people to demand solutions to the problems of climate change and nuclear warfare. Such an encounter will tell us we live in an interconnected world and must therefore devise new approaches to managing international relations that rely on cooperation rather than the unilateral exercise of power. A heart that fills with divine love tells us that we

11. Vermes, *Christian Beginnings*, 134–35.

are all equal in God's eyes, which encourages us to work toward creating a more inclusive society. A heart grounded in boundless love tells us there is more to life than material consumption, which makes it easier to support needed solutions to the problem of income inequality. The example of Jesus inspires me to act on these impulses that flow from a heart overflowing with love. It is for these reasons I remain a Christian.

To review briefly, I have pointed out that biblical beliefs are a major factor causing the current war between Israel and Hamas. The anti-Semitism that has followed is also the result of biblical belief. Biblical belief has also been responsible for the treating of women as second-class citizens throughout the scope of Christian history, an unfortunate situation that still persists within evangelical congregations. Discrimination against homosexuals and the larger LGBTQ community also has its origin in biblical belief. The delay and difficulty our country has had passing legislation to deal with climate change is due to the fact that most conservative Christians believe the two creation stories in Genesis are literally true. If temperatures are rising, that is due to God's action, not the irresponsible behavior of human beings. Finally, a major cause of economic inequality in this country is because Jesus' message of sharing wealth was hijacked by the early church. These are significant problems that Christians should not sweep under the rug.

I struggled through many classics during my years in high school English. Most of those novels I have long forgotten, with the exception of A Tale of Two Cities by Charles Dickens. Dickens opens the novel with these riveting words:

> It was the best of times, it was the worst of times, it was the age of wisdom, it was the age of foolishness, it was the epoch of belief, it was the epoch of incredulity, it was the season of Light, it was the season of Darkness, it was the spring of hope, it was the winter of despair.[12]

Dickens published A Tale of Two Cities in 1859, and the quotation cited above speaks as clearly to our situation today as

---

12. "Tale of Two Cities," para 3.

it did to the time of Dickens's novel. Artificial intelligence and an enlightened form of capitalism can end global hunger once and for all. Climate change can be managed safely by emerging technology and small lifestyle changes that allow a sustainable economy to emerge. Nuclear weapons can be defanged and replaced by safer strategies for managing international relations. The best of times!

Sadly, the current trajectory of world affairs is not so hopeful. Predatory capitalism seems to be the global paradigm, with people demanding more and more goods to consume. The technology is here, but the will of people to reduce their carbon footprint is lacking. The threat that nuclear weapons pose to the survival of the planet is off the radar screen of most of the world's citizens. Economic inequality continues to grow. Social media fosters separation, hatred, and threats of violence against people who appear to be different or threatening. The worst of times stands out as a real possibility.

But there are more than two billion Christians living in the world today. Imagine if more and more of them moved away from a religion of ideological belief and became followers of Jesus. Imagine if more and more Christians organized their lives around the messages stemming from a heart overflowing with divine love. Let the best of times roll!

Bibliography

Allison, Dale C., Jr. *The Historical Christ and the Theological Jesus.* Grand Rapids: Eerdmans, 2009.

Aslan, Reza. *Zealot: The Life and Times of Jesus of Nazareth.* New York: Random House, 2014.

Black, David Alan, ed. *Perspectives on the Ending of Mark.* Nashville: Broadman and Holman, 2008.

Borg, Marcus J. *Meeting Jesus Again for the First Time.* San Francisco: HarperOne, 2009.

Bushby, Joshua. "Why Climate Change Matters More Than Anything Else," *Foreign Affairs* 97.4 (Jul.-Aug. 2018) 49–57.

Carroll, James. *Constantine's Sword.* New York: Houghton Mifflin, 2001.

Carter, Warren. *Jesus and the Empire of God: Reading the Gospels in the Roman Empire.* Eugene, OR: Cascade Books, 2021.

Crossan, John Dominic. *The Historical Jesus.* San Francisco: HarperOne, 1992.

———. and Jonathan L. Reed. *Excavating Jesus: Beneath the Stones and Behind the Texts.* San Francisco: HarperCollins, 2001.

Damasio, Antonio. *Descartes' Error: Emotion, Reason and the Human Brain.* New York: Penguin, 2005.

Dreher, Diane. *The Tao of Inner Peace,* rev. ed. New York: Penguin Random House, 2000.

Ehrman, Bart D. *The New Testament: A Historical Introduction to Early Christian Writing.* New York: Oxford University Press, 1997.

———. *Misquoting Jesus: The Story Behind Who Changed the Bible and Why.* San Francisco: HarperCollins, 2005.

———. *How Jesus Became God: The Exaltation of a Jewish Preacher from Galilee.* San Francisco: HarperOne, 2014.

———. *Jesus: Apocalyptic Prophet for the New Millennium.* New York: Oxford University Press, 1999.

Emmons, Robert. *Thanks!: How Practicing Gratitude Can Make You Happier.* New York: Houghton Mifflin, 2007.

Flannery, Francis, and Rodney A. Werline, eds. *The Bible in Political Debate.* New York: Bloomsbury, 2012.

Fox, Matthew. *Christian Mystics: 365 Readings and Meditations*. Novato, CA: New World Library, 2011.

Fredriksen, Paula. *From Jesus to Christ: The Origins of the New Testament Images of Jesus*. New Haven: Yale University Press, 2008.

———. *Jesus of Nazareth: King of the Jews*. New York: Knopf, 1999.

Frishberg, Hannah. "American Church Attendance Hits Historic Low, Says Gallup Survey." *New York Post*, Mar. 31, 2021.

Funk, Robert W., Roy W. Hoover, and the Jesus Seminar. *The Five Gospels: What Did Jesus Really Say*. San Francisco: HarperCollins, 1993.

Galston, David. *Embracing the Human Jesus: A Wisdom Path for Contemporary Christianity*. Salem, OR: Polebridge, 2012.

Good, Jack. *The Dishonest Church*. Scotts Valley, CA: Rising Star, 2003.

Grudem, Wayne. *Politics according to the Bible*. Grand Rapids: Zondervan, 2010.

Herrick, Rick. *The Case Against Evangelical Christianity*. Cambridge, MA: Charles River, 2011.

———. *Moving Beyond Belief: A New Focus for the Christian Faith*. Eugene, OR: Wipf and Stock, 2022.

Herzog, William R., II. *Prophet and Teacher: An Introduction to the Historical Jesus*. Louisville: John Knox, 2005.

History.com editors. "Rwandan Genocide," History.com, Oct. 14, 2009. https://www.history.com/topics/africa/rwandan-genocide.

Horsley, Richard A. *Galilee: History, Politics, People*. Valley Forge, PA: Trinity, 1995.

Jenkins, Philip. *Jesus Wars*. San Francisco: HarperCollins, 2010.

Krieg, Carl. "The Birth and Death of the Church in the First Century." Progressing Spirit, Nov. 10, 2022. https://progressingspirit.com/2022/11/10/the-birth-and-death-of-the-church-in-the-first-century-part-1/.

———. "The Story of Jesus." ProgressiveChristianity.org, Feb. 17, 2023. https://progressivechristianity.org/resource/the-story-of-jesus/.

———. "Jesus and Wealth." ProgressiveChristianity.org, May 28, 2023.

MacCulloch, Diarmaid. *Christianity: The First Three Thousand Years*. New York: Viking, 2009.

McDowell, Josh. *The New Evidence That Demands a Verdict*. Nashville: Thomas Nelson, 1999.

Metaxas, Eric. *Bonhoeffer: Pastor, Martyr, Prophet, Spy*. Nashville: Nelson, 2010.

Rubenstein, Richard E. *When Jesus Became God: The Struggle to Define Christianity during the Last Days of Rome*. San Diego: Harcourt, 1999.

"The Rwandan Genocide." United States Holocaust Memorial Museum. https://encyclopedia.ushmm.org/content/en/article/the-rwanda-genocide

Smietana, Bob. "Thousands of Churches Close Every Year. What Will Happen to their Buildings?" *Religion News Service*, Mar. 15, 2022. https://religionnews.com/2022/03/15/thousands-of-churches-close-every-year-what-will-happen-to-their-buildings/.

Smith, Rick. "Why Plug Power, Sun Power, and Brookfield Renewable Stocks All Dropped Today." *Motley Fool*, Feb. 5, 2024.

Swimme, Brian. *The Universe Story: From the Primordial Flaring Forth to the Ecozoic Era—A Celebration of the Unfolding Cosmos*. San Francisco: HarperOne, 1994.

"A Tale of Two Cities." https://en.wikipedia.org/wiki/A_Tale_of_Two_Cities.

Thames, Knox. "Putin Is After More Than Land—He Wants the Religious Soul of Ukraine." *Religion News Service*, Feb. 24, 2022. https://religionnews. com/2022/02/24/putin-is-after-more-than-land-he-wants-the-religious-soul-of-ukraine/.

Tornicelli, Andrea. "The Statistics on the Slow Evaporation of European Christianity." Mercator, May 30, 2018. https://www.mercatornet.com/the-statistics-on-the-slow-evaporation-of-european-christianity.

Vermes, Geza. *Christian Beginnings: From Nazareth to Nicea*. New Haven Yale University Press, 2012.

———. *The Authentic Gospel of Jesus*. London: Penguin, 2003.

———. *Jesus the Jew*. Minneapolis: Fortress, 1981.

Vosper, Gretta. *With or without God*. Toronto: Harper Perennial, 2008.

Wallis, Jim. *God's Politics: Why the Right Gets It Wrong*. New York: Harper Collins, 2006.

"What Does Spirituality Mean to Us?: A Study of Spirituality in the United States Since Covid." Fetzer Institute, Nov. 30, 2023. https://spiritualitystudy. fetzer.org/.

Williams, Tarah, Andrew Bloeser, and Brian Harward. "Large Numbers of Americans Want a Strong, Rough, Anti-democratic Leaders." The Conversation, Dec. 30, 2023. https://theconversation.com/large-numbers-of-americans-want-a-strong-rough-anti-democratic-leader-198578.

Printed in Great Britain
by Amazon

57551605R00056